Shipwrecks

Titles in the Man-Made Disasters series include:

Airplane Crashes

Nuclear Accidents

Oil and Chemical Spills

Shipwrecks

Tragedies of Space Exploration

MAN-MADE
DISASTERS

Shipwrecks

Hillary Mayell

LUCENT
BOOKS ®

THOMSON
GALE

c.1

San Diego • Detroit • New York • San Francisco • Cleveland • New Haven, Conn. • Waterville, Maine • London • Munich

LIBRARY OF CONGRESS CATALOGING-IN-PUBLICATION DATA

Mayell, Hillary.
  Shipwrecks / by Hillary Mayell.
    p. cm. — (Manmade disasters)
Includes bibliographical references and index.
Summary: A historical look at shipwrecks, their causes, survival, how accidents happen,
investigations and prevention of shipwrecks.

  ISBN 1-59018-058-5 (hardback : alk. paper)
  1. Ship Accidents—Juvenile literature. I. Mayell, Hillary. II. Title. III. Series.
  TL553.5.M 335 2004
  363.12'465—dc21

Printed in the United States of America

Contents

Foreword 6

INTRODUCTION
Peril at Sea 8

CHAPTER ONE
The Ship Goes Down 13

CHAPTER TWO
Surviving a Catastrophe 28

CHAPTER THREE
How Accidents Happen 46

CHAPTER FOUR
Investigations at Sea 63

CHAPTER FIVE
Preventing Shipwrecks 79

Notes 96
Glossary 99
For Further Reading 101
Works Consulted 103
Index 107
Picture Credits 111
About the Author 112

Foreword

In the late 1990s a University of Florida study came to a surprising conclusion. Researchers determined that the local residents they surveyed were more afraid of nuclear accidents, chemical spills, and other man-made disasters than they were of natural disasters such as hurricanes and floods. This finding seemed especially odd given that natural disasters are often much more devastating than man-made disasters, at least in terms of human lives. The collapse of the two World Trade Center towers on September 11, 2001, was among the worst human-caused disasters in recent memory, yet even its horrific death toll of roughly three thousand pales in comparison to, for example, the 1976 earthquake in China that killed an estimated seven hundred thousand people.

How then does one explain people's overarching fear of man-made disasters? One factor mentioned by the Florida researchers related to the widespread perception that natural hazards are "acts of God" that no one can control. Earthquakes, forest fires, and the like are thus accepted as inevitable. Man-made disasters are viewed differently, as unpredictable yet maddeningly preventable. Even worse, because these new technologies are so incredibly complex—a 747 airliner has 6 million parts, the 100-foot-long control room of a nuclear power plant has thousands of gauges and controls—the root cause of the disaster can often be shockingly trivial. One notorious 1972 airliner crash occurred when a tiny lightbulb, the indicator for whether the nose landing gear was down, burned out. While in flight, the captain, copilot, and engineer decided to replace the bulb. With the crew distracted, someone in the cockpit accidentally disengaged the autopilot and the plane flew into the ground, killing 98 of 176 onboard.

Man-made disasters are also distressing because they are so furtive in their deadliness. The hazardous radiation emitted by the nuclear accident at Tokaimura, Japan, in 1999 could neither be seen nor smelled, and the lethal gas that leaked from a Union Carbide pesticide factory in India in 1984 settled silently over the city of Bhopal, killing thousands in their homes.

Another factor may be the widespread perception that man-made disasters are much worse than ever. This is probably true although faulty designs and shoddy workmanship have been causing building collapses, dam failures, and ship sinkings for thousands of years. Beginning with the twentieth century, what is new is industrial technology, such as nuclear power and oil refining, that can affect huge areas over many years when something goes wrong. The radiation from the disaster at the Chernobyl nuclear power plant in 1986 spread worldwide and has closed local areas to human habitation to this day. Finally, man-made disasters have begun to compound each other: In January 1997, a massive oil spill caused by the shipwreck of a Russian tanker in the Sea of Japan threatened to clog crucial cooling systems in nearby nuclear power plants.

Fortunately, humanity can learn vital lessons from man-made disasters. Practical insights mean that ocean liners no longer ply the seas, as the *Titanic* did, with too few lifeboats and no ability to see in the dark. Nuclear power plants are not being built with the type of tin-can containment building that Chernobyl had. The latest generation of oil tankers has double hulls, which should vastly reduce oil spills. On the more philosophical level man-made disasters offer valuable insights into issues relating to progress and technology, risk and safety, and government and corporate responsibility.

The Man-Made Disasters series presents a clear and up-to-date overview of such dramatic events as airplane crashes, nuclear accidents, oil and chemical spills, tragedies of space exploration, shipwrecks, and building collapses. Each book in the series serves as both a wide-ranging introduction and a guide to further study. Fully documented primary and secondary source quotes enliven the narrative. Sidebars highlight important events, personalities, and technologies. Annotated bibliographies provide readers with ideas for further research. Finally, the many facts and unforgettable stories relate the hubris—pride bordering on arrogance—as well as the resiliency of daring pioneers, bold innovators, brave rescuers, and lucky survivors.

Peril at Sea

It was bitter cold, with what crew members described as the smell of ice in the air, when the *Titanic*, the largest and most luxurious ship in the world, steamed through the North Atlantic on the night of April 15, 1912. Captain Edward Smith had hopes of making the ship's maiden voyage, from Southampton, England, to New York City, in excellent time. He had the ship running at twenty-two knots (roughly twenty-five miles per hour), close to top speed. The night was moonless, the skies clear, and the water calm, but an unseen field of ice loomed ahead.

Shortly before midnight, Frederick Fleet, a lookout high up in the ship's crow's nest, suddenly spotted a dark object directly in the path of the ship. He urgently warned the bridge: "Iceberg, right ahead!"[1] The berg had also been seen from the bridge, and orders were quickly given to reverse the engines and make a hard turn to the starboard (right) in an attempt to avoid the low-lying mountain of ice. The turn could not be made fast enough, however, and the *Titanic* scraped her side along the iceberg. Although not a dramatic crash, it was to be the ship's death sentence.

An inspection determined almost immediately that the damage the ship had sustained was catastrophic. At first, to avert panic, the officers and crew members downplayed the threat, and it took some time for passengers to realize the seriousness of what had happened. Many were reluctant to get into the lifeboats. They looked at the long drop down to the sea, viewed the endless stretch of black water, and registered the freezing cold temperatures. Then they considered the huge ship on which they were standing, apparently solid and brightly lit, with a reputation for being unsinkable. And many decided to wait and see. The first lifeboat was not lowered to the sea until 12:45 A.M., an hour after impact. Even then, with

a capacity of sixty-five, only twenty-five people had been convinced to abandon ship.

The *Titanic* steams out of Southampton, England, on April 10, 1912, for its first—and last—voyage.

Over the next thirty minutes all that changed. The ship began to list noticeably, and people panicked. Children were separated from parents, and husbands from wives, as the urgency of the situation became clear. The command was given to abandon ship; women and children were loaded into the boats first. Only slowly did the realization dawn that not only was the ship going to sink, but there were not enough lifeboats to save everyone. Even with a life jacket, no one could last long in the icy water. As the ship's bow (front) tilted more and more toward the bottom of the sea, the stern arched high into the night sky. People grabbed anything that would keep them from sliding down the deck. Many jumped into the water to avoid being pulled under by the suction the ship would create when it finally went down. At 2:20 A.M. the *Titanic* broke in half and disappeared beneath the water. Survivor Eva Hart remembered the moment vividly:

> The stern stuck up in the ocean for what seemed to me like a long time . . . then keeled over and went down. You could hear the people thrashing about and screaming and drowning. I remember saying to my mother once, "How dreadful that noise was," and I'll always remember her

▼ Passengers on the imperiled *Vestris* struggle to don life preservers and board lifeboats.

reply: "Yes, but think about the silence that followed it". . . because all of a sudden the ship wasn't there, the lights weren't there, and the cries weren't there. Silence. The silence was worse.[2]

Of the twenty-two hundred passengers and crew onboard, more than fifteen hundred died.

Recipe for Disaster

The sinking of the *Titanic* served as a major wake-up call for marine safety. Investigations into the reasons for the disaster led to various practical recommendations, including requirements that passenger ships carry enough lifeboats to accommodate everyone onboard during an emergency, and that an international ice patrol service be established. Subsequent shipwrecks prompted further reforms. The November 12, 1928, sinking of the *Vestris*, a British passenger steamer, in heavy seas two hundred miles off the coast of Virginia, dramatized the need for better life preservers. Rescuers noted that many of the 128 people found floating dead in the water were wearing life jackets but had drowned because when they lost consciousness due to the cold water, the life jacket kept them floating, but facedown. Maritime companies eventually developed better life preservers with flotation angles and self-righting properties that could keep a floating person's head above water.

Despite the improved technology and better safety regulations, ships both prominent and obscure continue to collide, sink, run aground, and catch on fire with regularity, at a cost of thousands of lives every year. The most well-intentioned reforms can go only so far—laws stipulate that ships carry life preservers, for example, but the U.S. Coast Guard says that about 80 percent of the victims in fatal boating accidents did not bother to wear them. Similarly, all the high-tech navigational technology in the world is worthless if, as all too often happens, ship owners and captains do not ensure that it is used.

Many things can go wrong with ships at sea, and if they do go wrong, the scale of the disaster can be huge because of the increased size of modern ships and the thousands of passengers some carry. Unfortunately, notes Yale sociology professor Charles Perrow, any single reform or new technology is unlikely to be a panacea for preventing future shipwrecks. In his groundbreaking book, *Normal Accidents: Living with High-Risk Technologies*, he says:

> The safe, well-designed Shell tanker can still be rammed by an itinerant cargo ship with a long list of violations; better radio communication can mean less communication because of the chatter; collision avoidance systems are swamped by higher speeds; larger tankers, which would

reduce occasions for arrivals and departures where the biggest danger lie, mean more and bigger explosions because of mysterious processes inside the huge tanks.[3]

Statistics on ship losses collected by the London-based Lloyd's insurance company suggest that the odds are about one in fifteen that a one-hundred-ton or larger ship with a life expectancy of thirty years will be lost, from sinking, fire, or other disaster, before it is retired. Clearly, the risk of disaster at sea can never be completely eliminated. Even so, the insights humanity has gained from many millennia of shipwrecks, as well as from heroic rescues at sea, can offer valuable lessons for the future.

CHAPTER ONE

The Ship Goes Down

Around sixty thousand years ago, small groups of modern humans became the first explorers, leaving Africa to colonize the rest of the world. At least some heard the call of the sea, for archaeological evidence suggests humans had reached Australia by fifty thousand years ago. The early travelers in all likelihood followed the southern coastline of Asia, built rafts, and traveled the roughly 155 miles across the open sea. Humans have been crossing the world's oceans, traveling up rivers, and plying the waters of lakes and bays, ever since.

Shipbuilding has evolved considerably since those first explorers made their trip. But seafarers bent on trade, exploration, and finding new lands to conquer continued to face tremendous risks. Little was known of the geography of waterways and coastlines, the ability to predict a storm was limited, and vessels were built of lashed-together reeds or hollowed-out logs. If catastrophe struck and the ship sank, there was little hope of rescue.

Small wooden crafts powered by oars were eventually succeeded by ships using the wind to move them across the water. By the late nineteenth century, sails had become all but obsolete, replaced by steam. Iron and steel took over for wood, allowing ships to be built on a much bigger scale, carrying larger cargoes and more passengers. But traveling the seas remained fraught with danger, and shipwreck was a constant threat.

At the Mercy of Wind and Weather

The ominous names sailors have given various coastlines tell the story of the enormous challenges early ocean-going travelers faced when they embarked on a trip. Tricky shorelines, uncharted reefs and shoals, storms, fog, and unseen currents have combined to earn coastlines monikers such as "Grave-yard of the Atlantic" (North Carolina) and "The Martyrs" (the Florida Keys) because of the many ships that foundered there. In Africa, the coastline along Namibia is known as "Skeleton Coast." More than three thousand ships have been reported sunk between there and the "Wild Coast" in South Africa.

The sad final journey of the *General Grant* illustrates how much early ships were at the mercy of the wind and the weather. The three-masted sailing ship left Melbourne, Australia, in May 1866 carrying eighty-three passengers and crew, along with a cargo of wool and gold. The captain was skilled, and the wind steady. The ship made good time during the first week of its voyage, heading toward the vast expanse of the South Pacific, ultimately intending to round South America's Cape Horn and cross the Atlantic to London. But the remote reefs and uninhabited islands of the Indian Ocean south of New Zealand were poorly charted, and little was known about the ocean currents. After two days of bad weather, the ship emerged from a thick fog with the towering black cliffs of Auckland Island dead ahead. The wind dropped, and the ship drifted toward the wall with no way of stopping. After hitting the cliff, the ship drifted into a huge cavern, coming to a stop when the tallest mast scraped the ceiling. When the tide rose, the masts were plunged down through the hull and the *General Grant* quickly sank. Lifeboats were launched, but in the confusion sixty-eight people drowned.

Fifteen survivors rowed for two days and two nights before reaching Disappointment Island. With the last of their matches they managed to get a fire lit, which they kept going for the next year and a half. In January 1867 four men left in a lifeboat, intending to reach New Zealand. They disappeared without a trace. Illness claimed another survivor. Only ten of those who set sail on the *General Grant* remained alive by the time a seal-ing expedition finally discovered them in November 1867.

In addition to typhoons, snowstorms, hurricanes, heavy seas, and winds that can travel at one hundred miles per hour, rogue waves towering ninety feet high can appear out of nowhere. These freak waves, which sometimes occur in calm seas, are large enough to capsize even the largest of modern ships. In 1942 a giant wave hit the mammoth liner *Queen Mary*, then transporting fifteen thousand soldiers, about seven hundred miles west of Scotland. The force of the wave rolled the huge ocean liner almost onto its side. Fortunately no passengers were lost, and the ship righted itself and completed its voyage to England. More recently, in June 1984, the *Marques,* a three-masted sail-training ship built in 1917, was sunk by such a wave during a tall ships race off the coast of Bermuda. Only nine of twenty-eight onboard survived.

Unsinkable: The Ultimate Folly

Foul weather and rogue waves are beyond human control but many other factors leading to shipwrecks are not. These include commercial pressures, overconfidence in technology, poor communication, shoddy construction materials, and flawed designs. Any one of these factors on its own can lead to disaster. When they combine, as they did to cause perhaps the most famous human-made disaster of the twentieth century, the sinking of the *Titanic,* the tragic outcome takes on an air of inevitability.

Titanic captain Smith was intent on reaching New York ahead of schedule. Despite the fact that the *Titanic* had received several warnings throughout the day from other ships

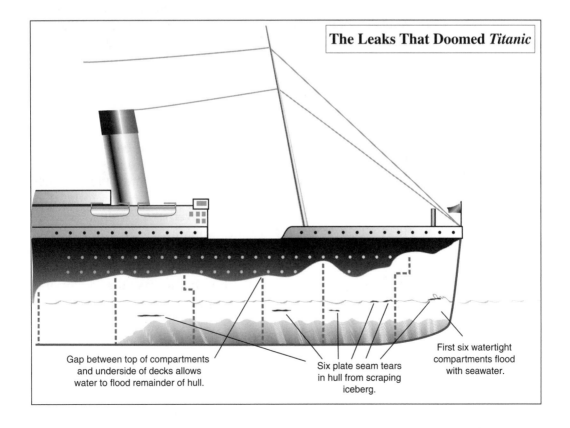

The Leaks That Doomed *Titanic*

Gap between top of compartments and underside of decks allows water to flood remainder of hull.

Six plate seam tears in hull from scraping iceberg.

First six watertight compartments flood with seawater.

HOW TO SIGNAL "HELP!"

When wireless on transatlantic ships became more common at the beginning of the twentieth century, many ships from different countries each had their own way of signaling that they were in trouble. British operators, due to their experience as railroad and telegraph operators, used the general call for all stations to pay attention, "CQ," and added a "D" on the end to signal distress. Thus the emergency code CQD does not come, as sometimes claimed, from "come quick danger."

Nor does SOS stand for "save our ship" or "send out succor." An international conference adopted these letters as a distress signal in 1906 primarily because the radio code of three dots, three dashes, and three dots was easy to send and to understand. Stations hearing this distress call were to immediately cease handling traffic and respond until the emergency was over. In the years following the sinking of the *Titanic*, SOS gradually replaced CQD. By the early 1930s the spoken term "Mayday," stemming from the French *m'aider*, meaning "help me," had become the widely recognized call given when a ship or plane was in immediate danger.

in the area about ice, the ship was traveling at close to its top speed. When the bridge officers expressed concern about the likelihood of encountering icebergs and ice fields, Smith reduced the ship's speed by only half a knot. All told, six warnings about ice ahead were received that day. Communication on the ship was such that not all were delivered to the captain, and he posted only one in the chartroom. He did not alert the officers on the bridge that there had been several others.

Not yet recognized as a safety feature, wireless radio was one of the many luxury services available to passengers on the *Titanic*. Wireless access allowed people to stay in touch with those on shore, much like Internet access today. On ships, "Wireless was initially perceived as a frivolity," according to historian John Maxtone-Graham, "a reassurance to passengers who might want the latest refinement."[4] The *Titanic* had just two wireless operators, and the radio set had broken down earlier in the day. By the time it was up and working again, the backlog of passenger messages was huge, and the ship was close enough to Newfoundland's Cape Race, the easternmost point of North America, to once again be within range of operators.

Jack Phillips, the *Titanic*'s wireless operator on duty that night, was overwhelmed with work. At around 9:30 P.M. he received an ice report from another ship, giving position co-ordinates and stating: "Ice report. Saw much heavy pack ice and great number large icebergs, also field ice. Weather good, clear."[5] Phillips, overwhelmed by the backlog, went back to working through the pile of passenger messages, which were given priority. The ice warning went undelivered. A little later, another message, this time from the nearby *Californian*, broke in: "Say, old man, we are surrounded by ice and stopped." Phillips, overworked, tired, and angry, wired back, "Shut up! Shut up! I am busy, I am working Cape Race!"[6] The stage was set for disaster, one that Phillips himself would not survive.

A Deadly Scrape

Something as seemingly inconsequential as the *Titanic*'s riv-ets might have also contributed to the mighty ship's downfall. The Scottish company that made the iron for the 3 million riv-ets used in building the *Titanic* had too many projects and not enough skilled workers to meet its commitments. "The iron went out the door with four times the normal percentage of slag inclusions [impurities], and there was no good quality control method to counter this problem at the time," writes James R. Chiles in *Inviting Disaster: Lessons from the Edge of Technology*. He adds:

> The slag made the rivet heads more prone to shear off un-der the grazing collision that the *Titanic* suffered, opening the hull at plate seams. We know from undersea observa-tions that the ship sustained neither giant rip nor gash; in-stead the size of all the openings, taken together, was about the square footage of a throw rug.[7]

The poor-quality rivets allowed plate seams on the hull to separate when the ship grazed the iceberg. The *Titanic* liter-ally came apart at the seams. Water began to flood six of the liner's thirteen separate hull compartments. The ship's de-signers had made a major miscalculation, however. Rather than being watertight, the interior walls of these compart-ments did not reach up to the underside of the lowest decks. Thus water could flow from one compartment to the next, which indeed is what happened, causing the ship to sink quite rapidly.

Another equipment-related factor had been born of arro-gance. The liner's designers and the directors of the ship's

▶ This grimly prophetic photo of a lifeboat and the *Titanic*'s bridge, with captain Edward Smith peering down from the very top, was taken just before the ship left England.

company, the venerable White Star Line, considered the ship so safe as to be virtually unsinkable. Alexander Carlisle, a managing director of the shipyard that built the *Titanic*, had presented the directors with a plan for forty-eight lifeboats capable of holding a total of 2,886 persons. His plan was rejected on the grounds of expense. "We spent two hours discussing carpet for the First Class cabins and fifteen minutes discussing lifeboats,"[8] he later said. Thus the *Titanic* left port carrying twenty lifeboats with a seating capacity of 1,178 for the 2,207 people onboard the ship. This was actually 10 percent above the number required by law at the time.

Fearful Ferries

The actions of cavalier captains, shoddy shipbuilders, and arrogant owners continue to plague sea travel. Huge ocean-going liners and the more numerous luxury passenger cruise ships, however, are now chock full of the best maritime technology money can buy, and thus are very unlikely to be victimized by *Titanic*-scale disasters. Rather, in recent years the all-too-human operation of ferries has caused the high fatalities from today's shipwrecks. In Europe and the Middle East, so-called roll-on/roll-off ("ro-ro") passenger and vehicle ferries have accounted for a number of notable disasters. These ships have cargo doors that open in the bow and stern that allow for easy loading and unloading of autos and people. This same flow-through design, however, can also let a ro-ro sink very quickly following an accident at sea.

A typical incident occurred on December 16, 1991, in the Middle East. Captain Hassan Moro, a widely respected seaman who had taught at the Egyptian Naval Academy, began his normal return trip crossing the Red Sea from Saudi Arabia to Egypt in the *Salem Express*. The ferry was loaded with up to sixteen hundred passengers, many dressed in the flowing robes of pilgrims returning from Mecca. Because Moro was so familiar with the route, he usually took a shortcut that hugged the coastline. Other captains avoided the route because it came too close to dangerous reefs. But the shortcut saved two hours, and that night the ship was being battered by high seas and gale force winds. Moro decided that the shortcut, being closer to shore, would also provide some protection from the storm.

Unfortunately, darkness and the storm reduced visibility to zero, and the ship hit a reef. The impact punched a hole in the hull and also jolted one of the cargo doors, allowing water to rush onto the car deck. The double breach sank the *Salem Express* within twenty minutes, too fast to launch lifeboats. The storm was so intense that boats anchored safely in a harbor nearby were unable to launch any rescue attempts. Only 180 people survived. (The official death toll of 470 is widely regarded as much too low.)

The Overcrowded "Floating Coffins"

Similarly lethal sinkings in recent years have occurred on local ferries plying rivers, lakes, and coastal waters in much of the developing world. Sometimes derided as "floating coffins" for their safety records, these are often antiquated passenger ships that have been decommissioned in the United States, Japan, or elsewhere only to be pressed into service in poorer countries such as Haiti and Bangladesh. Factors such as haphazard industry inspection and government regulation frequently let these ships go to sea overcrowded, badly maintained, and poorly staffed. This has contributed to catastrophes of staggering proportions—as many as five hundred people lost when the ferry *Neptune* capsized off the coast of Haiti in 1993, up to one thousand dead in 1996 when the Tanzanian ferry *Bukoba* capsized on Lake Victoria, and more than five hundred thought to have died on June 29, 2000, when an overloaded ferry capsized in a storm off the coast of Sulawesi, an Indonesian island.

An Asian ferry accident ranks as history's worst peacetime shipwreck. In December 1987 the *Dona Paz* was typical of the many ferries transporting passengers among the more than seven thousand islands of the Philippines. While moving through the Tablas Strait between Mindoro and Panay Islands, the ferry collided with the *Victor*, a small oil tanker carrying 370,000 gallons of oil. The impact caused a fire, which quickly spread. Burning oil from the tanker soon blanketed the sea.

▼ Philippine citizens check a posting for information on the sinking of the *Dona Paz* ferry.

Roughly forty-five hundred people died as the water became a flaming inferno. Legally, the ship was allowed to carry only about two thousand passengers.

Despite calls for more oversight, ferry tragedies in the developing world have continued in recent years. In Bangladesh, for instance, a country crossed by more than two hundred rivers, ferries are a key mode of transportation. Frequently dangerously overcrowded, more than four thousand people have died in about 260 accidents since 1977. In July 2003 an overcrowded ferry transporting some 750 people from Bangladesh's capital city of Dhaka to the southern Bhola district sank near the terminal. Six hundred passengers and crew died in the monsoon-swollen river waters. One estimate is that fifteen hundred people die on Asian ferries every year.

Warships Take Their Toll

The ongoing death toll on ro-ros and overcrowded passenger ferries is dreadful but the marine disasters that have claimed by far the most lives have occurred as a result of acts of war. History's most disastrous sinkings, in fact, happened during World War II. Never before had so many people been able to crowd onto such large vessels that could be attacked with so much devastating force. Horrific death tolls occurred not only on battleships (2,498 Japanese sailors died when a blizzard of American fighters and bombers sank the *Yamato* on April 7, 1945), aircraft carriers (on June 19, 1944, 1,650 Japanese sailors died onboard the *Taiho* after it was sunk by the U.S. submarine *Albacore*), and other warships. German, Japanese, and Allied troop transport and refugee ships accounted for a half dozen sinkings, each of which claimed in excess of five thousand victims. The liner *Lancastria*, for example, was full of British troops being evacuated from German-occupied France in June 1940 when it was sunk by German planes. Estimates for the number of British soldiers killed range from three to seven thousand. The official British report on the sinking is being kept sealed for one hundred years, so the true death toll may become known in 2040.

The greatest maritime disasters to date occurred in the waning months of World War II. After a long and bloody defense of their homeland from Nazi German attack, by late 1944 the Russian army was on the offense and had reached German-occupied territories. Many terrified German citizens,

SINK THE *BISMARCK*!

Two major warships went down in one of the great naval battles of World War II. It was fought in May 1941, when the British *Hood* and *Prince of Wales* encountered the famous German battleship *Bismarck* in the Atlantic off the coast of Iceland. Newly launched and considered by the Germans as almost invincible, with its powerful engines and massive guns, the *Bismarck* scored a direct hit on the *Hood*, causing a huge explosion that sank the battle cruiser, taking 1,383 men with her. But the *Bismarck* also suffered damage during the battle, causing it to head for the safety of the French coast. Three days later, after a fierce two-hour battle with British warplanes, battleships, and cruisers, the *Bismarck* capsized and sank, with the loss of all but 110 of her crew of some 2,300 men.

▲ Soldiers and officials of Nazi Germany gathered in February 1939 to celebrate the launch of the completed hull of the battleship *Bismarck*.

mostly women, children, and the elderly, fled as the Russian army approached. When some of these refugees reached Danzig (now Gdansk, Poland) on the Baltic Sea, they were put on boats and transported to points farther west. All told, 2 million Germans were evacuated in the final months of the war. But not all made it to safety.

On January 30, 1945, the *Wilhelm Gustloff*, a modern German liner built during the 1930s, was loaded with perhaps as many as ten thousand passengers as it ventured out of the Bay of Danzig. (The exact number is not known, due to the chaos of wartime evacuation.) These were primarily German families fleeing the advancing Russian troops, but hundreds of injured German soldiers were also onboard. The ship was struck by three torpedoes fired at close range by the Soviet submarine *S-13*. All but about twelve hundred onboard died as the *Gustloff* rapidly went down in the frigid water. Perhaps half of the nine thousand dead were children and infants.

Eleven days later, in the same area, the same sub torpedoed the German *General Steuben*. The converted passenger ship sank in just seven minutes with the loss of an estimated three thousand lives. Minutes before midnight on April 16, the Soviet sub *L-3* torpedoed the German *Goya*. The ship, which was carrying as many as six thousand people, broke in half almost immediately and sank in four minutes. Only 183 people survived. All told, in a three-month period, roughly eighteen thousand people, mostly women, children, and wounded soldiers, died in the icy waters of the Baltic Sea.

Danger on Land

High death tolls from marine accidents can also occasionally occur on land. Marine authorities received a graphic lesson in the potential for widespread disaster from a harbor accident on December 16, 1917. Early that morning, a Norwegian supply ship named *Imo* headed out of the harbor in Halifax, Nova Scotia, to make its way across the Atlantic. World War I was raging, and the *Mont Blanc*, a French ship carrying an enormous amount of explosives, headed in to the harbor to await an escort.

The two ships saw one another approaching. The *Mont Blanc* captain signaled the larger, faster ship that he was in the correct channel. The *Imo* signaled back that it was intending to move even farther into the *Mont Blanc's* channel. Despite several rounds of signaling back and forth, the two ships managed to collide—while the *Imo* was going full speed. The impact struck sparks and the *Mont Blanc* caught on fire. The crew immediately abandoned ship, rowing to shore and yelling warnings about the explosion they knew was about to happen.

The *Mont Blanc* drifted close enough to a pier to set it on fire. The fire department responded quickly, and crowds, drawn by the sight of the flaming ship, came down to the docks to watch. Shortly after nine, the *Mont Blanc* exploded, creating the biggest human-made explosion before the nuclear age. More than three hundred acres of the north end of Halifax were leveled. Windows shattered fifty miles away, and the *Mont Blanc*'s half-ton anchor was found two miles distant. The powerful explosion killed at least two thousand people and injured another nine thousand, about a thousand of them permanently. In May 1919 the Supreme Court of Canada determined that both ships were equally at fault.

The Halifax explosion remains the worst harbor accident to date but many marine authorities say that the potential for disaster has increased in recent years due to the development of massive tankers capable of carrying millions of gallons of

▼ Much of the Canadian port city of Halifax was devastated after a ship collision detonated a mammoth explosion in December 1917.

potentially toxic or explosive compounds. For example, nine-hundred-foot-long tankers filled with highly flammable liquefied natural gas routinely venture into Boston and other ports where the unloading facilities are located near urban areas. A Coast Guard study determined that the hypothetical accidental release of highly toxic chlorine gas, as it evaporated from even a small liquid chlorine tank that ruptured on a dock near New York City, could kill seventy-five thousand people. The terrorist attacks of September 11, 2001, added a new urgency to reducing the threat posed by such shipments. "The Coast Guard's job," notes writer H.D.S. Greenway, "is to make sure another Halifax doesn't happen in America, either because of accident or malice."[9]

▲ The March 1978 grounding of the *Amoco Cadiz* resulted in one of history's worst oil spills.

Environmental Mishaps

The destruction of much of Halifax in 1917 is an indication that the number of human deaths is not the only marker for measuring the extent of a shipwreck disaster. Today, however,

▲ Hand-washing of oil-covered birds and other wildlife is part of the extensive cleanup required after an oil spill.

it is often the natural rather than the man-made environment that is most threatened by offshore disasters. One of the earliest alarms was heard on March 18, 1967, when the *Torrey Canyon*, the first of the big supertankers, struck a reef off the coast of England, ran aground, and spilled some 36 million gallons of oil into the sea. It was the world's first major oil pollution disaster. Very little was known about how to clean up such a mess, and some of the methods used were more disastrous for marine life and wildlife than the oil itself would have been. The spill triggered international awareness of the magnitude of the potential catastrophes presented by supertankers, and led to changes in international law.

But change comes slowly. More than twenty years later, on March 24, 1989, the *Exxon Valdez* ran aground in Alaska's Prince William Sound. The 11 million gallons of oil that spilled and spread for the next two months affected thirteen hundred miles of shoreline—roughly the distance from New Jersey to South Carolina. It killed more than three hundred thousand seabirds, twenty-six hundred sea otters, three hundred harbor seals, and perhaps millions of fish. Moreover, as environmentally devastating as this spill was, it is not even in the top thirty of history's worst oil spill shipwrecks. That record goes to the July 19, 1979, collision of the *Atlantic Empress* and the *Aegean Captain*, which spilled more than 47 million gallons of crude oil into the waters of the Caribbean. Two weeks later, while the *Atlantic Empress* was being towed to port, the tanker spilled an additional 41 million gallons. This disaster occurred barely a year after the previous all-time worst, the wreck of the *Amoco Cadiz*, which spilled some 68 million gallons of oil off the coast of Brittany, France.

Although the immediate cause of many shipwrecks involving oil spills can be traced to onboard errors that cause a vessel to run aground or collide with another ship, the underlying cause often points to institutional factors relating to how oil tankers are operated and regulated. Laws requiring oil companies to pay for the environmental damage caused by oil spills have evolved slowly. A shipwreck that occurred on February 15, 1996, illustrates the problem. On that day, the tanker *Sea Empress* ran aground while attempting to enter the harbor of Milford Haven, Wales, at low tide. Over the next week, spilled crude oil came ashore along 125 miles of coastline, much of it national park land designated as being of international importance for its beauty and wildlife. The British newspaper the *Independent* summarized the problem of liability nicely when covering the disaster: "Built in Spain; owned by a Norwegian; registered in Cyprus; managed from Glasgow; chartered by the French; crewed by Russians; flying a Liberian flag; carrying an American cargo; and pouring oil on to the Welsh coast. But who takes the blame?"[10]

Questions about responsibility are crucial public issues, but when a shipwreck happens everyone onboard has a much more immediate concern: how to survive.

CHAPTER TWO

Surviving a Catastrophe

Surviving a shipwreck can depend on a host of factors: whether the accident took place in calm or stormy weather, and at night or during the day; the competence of the crew in an emergency; the availability and condition of lifesaving equipment; whether the ship actually sinks and if it does, how much time it takes to go under; and how quickly rescuers can reach victims. Even the temperature of the water can be crucial. The immense loss of life on the *Titanic*, for example, was a function of a combination of these factors. The accident occurred at night, there was a delay of almost an hour before the lifeboats—too few for the number of passengers —began to be loaded, the closest ships were several hours away, and the waters of the North Atlantic were frigid.

Such dire circumstances doomed about two-thirds of the *Titanic*'s passengers and crew, but seven hundred fortunate souls still managed to survive. Luck has long been a crucial ingredient for surviving a shipwreck, with recent advances in technologies and methods playing an increasingly important role in rescue efforts.

A Disaster Averted?

The sinking of the sleek Italian ocean liner *Andrea Doria* could have been a disaster of *Titanic* proportions if not for the remarkable success of the rescue efforts. A luxurious ship that offered travelers game rooms, three outdoor pools, original art, and elegant dining, the *Andrea Doria* was one day away from completing a successful run from its home port of Genoa, Italy, to New York City on July 25, 1956, when it ran into an early evening bank of fog. Captain Piero Calamai ordered the engine room to slightly reduce the liner's twenty-three-knot speed. In theory, he should have slowed down considerably, enough to come to a stop well within its range of visibility. But like many large-ship captains, he felt pressure to remain on schedule, and slowing down would delay the ship's arrival in New York.

Calamai felt confident about speeding through fog so thick that, at times, he could not see his own ship's bow from the bridge. Technology had changed since the time of the *Titanic*, and the *Andrea Doria* had top-of-the-line equipment. Instead of relying on lookouts when visibility was poor, radar used the reflection of radio waves to identify the location of distant ships. Boat design standards had also changed, and the eleven separate compartments in the *Andrea Doria*'s hull reached all the way to the underdecks, making the ship much more watertight than, for example, the *Titanic* had been. Launched on its maiden voyage just three years earlier, the newly built ship carried the most modern safety and navigational equipment available. Legislation following the *Titanic* disaster required liners to carry enough lifeboats to accommodate all passengers and crew, and the *Andrea Doria*'s lifeboats could carry two thousand people, more than enough for the 1,706 people onboard.

The ocean may seem vast, but the shipping lanes south of Nantucket, Massachusetts, on the approach to New York, are so busy sailors sometimes refer to the area as the "Times Square of the Atlantic." Calamai, a conscientious captain, stayed on the bridge as the *Andrea Doria* plied through the dense fog. He was there around 10:45 P.M. when another ship was spotted on the radar screen, seventeen miles away, heading directly toward them. Slowly, inexorably, the *Andrea Doria* and the Swedish liner *Stockholm* drew together, pulled almost as if by magnets. A series of small navigational miscalculations by the officers of both ships, and the failure of the *Stockholm* to signal its last turn, combined with deadly effect. At 11:10 P.M., instead of gliding past each other perilously close but unharmed, the *Stockholm* ripped into the *Andrea Doria* at full speed. "I could see a large shower of sparks and hear the crashing sound of shrieking metal as the *Stockholm* slammed into the starboard side of our ship. Immediately the floor tilted at a sharp angle," survivor Kathy Dickson later recalled.[11] Some forty *Andrea Doria* passengers were killed almost immediately as the bow of the *Stockholm* plowed thirty feet into the bowels of the *Andrea Doria*, leaving a gaping V-shaped hole upon backing out. The *Stockholm*'s bow was

▲ The bow of the Swedish liner *Stockholm* was sheared off when the ship collided with the *Andrea Doria* in July 1956.

sheared off. Even worse, the hole it left in the *Andrea Doria* extended above the ship's watertight compartments, ensuring an eventual sinking.

Nightmare at Sea

Linda Morgan, the fourteen-year-old daughter of radio announcer Edward Morgan, had gone to sleep in her berth onboard the *Andrea Doria* that night in cabin 52, which she shared with her eight-year-old half-sister Joan. Unsettled by the fog—her stepfather, a newspaperman, had joked at dinner about the ship crashing—Linda could not know that her sleep would soon be interrupted by a real-life nightmare. Awakened suddenly by the crash, she looked about to find her blankets missing and the ceiling of her cabin gone. Not knowing where she was, and frightened, she called for her mother. A sailor on the *Stockholm* who had been dispatched to inspect the damage to the smashed nose of the ship heard Linda. Climbing through the debris he found the teenager and carried her to the ship's hospital. Doctors there asked her her name, which they could not find on the ship's manifest, its list of passengers. After some moments of confusion, she was asked where she had come from. It was only when she answered "Madrid" that the doctors realized the impossible had happened—she was a passenger from the *Andrea Doria*.

A TRAGEDY AND A MIRACLE

Due to an oversight, Linda Morgan's name was not included on the list of the survivors aboard the *Stockholm*, and hundreds of newspapers reported her as one of the dead. When the damaged but still seaworthy *Stockholm*, the last ship carrying survivors, crept into New York at noon on July 27, the dock was crowded with anxious families who had not heard from missing loved ones. Edward Morgan, who had been told that someone onboard the *Andrea Doria* had seen Linda's body, was one of them. Hoping for a miracle, he boarded the *Stockholm* and was told that Linda was indeed alive and had been transferred to a hospital with a broken arm and two smashed kneecaps. Reporting to his listeners that night, Morgan described the collision of the *Andrea Doria* and the *Stockholm* as a story of "tragedy interspliced with the thread of happiness and even maybe miracle."

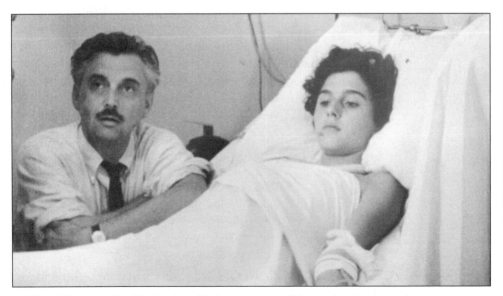

▲ Edward Morgan visits his daughter Linda, a survivor of the *Andrea Doria*, as she recovers in a New York City hospital.

The *Stockholm* had crashed directly into cabin 52 and the adjoining 54, which held Linda's mother and stepfather. Her stepfather was killed almost immediately, and her little sister was swept irretrievably out to sea. Linda's mother spent hours trapped in the wreckage of the cabins before eventually being evacuated from the *Andrea Doria*. Linda was lucky to be alive—the *Stockholm*'s bow had apparently entered right under her bed, scooped up her mattress, and carried her back with it.

In addition to Linda Morgan, the *Stockholm* had its own victims, and a severely damaged ship, to deal with. Five sailors in forward cabins had died or been mortally wounded in the impact, and the bow of the *Stockholm* was taking on water. The crew managed to save the ship by pumping almost a hundred tons of freshwater in forward tanks into the sea, righting the boat long enough for emergency repairs. The emergency was hardly over, however, as the two wounded ships faced each other in the dark night.

Desperate Hours

The situation for survivors back onboard the *Andrea Doria* was surprisingly desperate. As the ship rolled slightly to her side, more and more water continued to pour into the breached compartments. The list steadily grew throughout the night, seriously hampering the launching of lifeboats. Even more disturbing to the passengers, Captain Calamai decided not to make any announcements about what was going on. Beyond the initial instructions to collect their life jackets and go to assigned emergency muster stations, they heard not a word. In *Saved! The Story of the Andrea Doria*, William Hoffer described the wait.

> A dark apprehension snared the passengers. Would they succumb, one by one, until the ship rolled over and took its remaining victims swiftly? To many, it seemed that most of the *Andrea Doria* officers and crew members had disappeared into the same fog that cloaked the ship. They were human wreckage bobbing precariously close to the safety of New York Harbor, but agonizingly distant from immediate aid.[12]

Calamai testified at later inquiries that he wanted to avoid passenger panic. But as the ship's loudspeakers remained silent, the passengers felt abandoned. The frantic SOS that had been sent out was received by several ships in the area, but none big enough to accommodate anywhere close to the more than seventeen hundred people onboard the *Andrea Doria*. As the hours passed that dark and cold night, many passengers, hanging on to whatever was at hand to keep from sliding down the gradually tilting deck, felt that they were sitting there waiting to die.

Seemingly miraculously, several hours after the collision the fog lifted, and passengers were greeted by the sight of the *Ile de France*. After hearing the SOS, her captain, hardly believing that the *Andrea Doria* could really be sinking, had turned the huge passenger liner around and sped toward the collision. When the *Ile de France* arrived and aimed its spotlights at the scene of the disaster, lighting up the night, the captain was surprised and alarmed by the *Andrea Doria*'s extreme list.

A Perilous At-Sea Rescue

Despite the fact that the fog had lifted, the rescue efforts remained perilous. It was still dark, and the waters of the Atlantic are frigid. Because the *Andrea Doria* was listing to one side, half her lifeboats, the ones on the ship's high side, became inoperable. This left about one thousand lifeboat seats, not enough to accommodate everyone. Moreover, the

▼ A vacated *Andrea Doria* lists severely to starboard shortly before sinking to the bottom of the Atlantic.

lifeboats on the ship's low side now swung out too far to be boarded from the ship. The boats had to be lowered to the water, and then passengers either had to slide down a rope to reach them, or be trussed up in complicated rope swings and lowered. The first lifeboats to leave the deck of the *Andrea Doria* were only half full, and some carried mostly crew members who were abandoning the ship and leaving the passengers to fend for themselves.

As the *Andrea Doria* continued its slow roll, it created a suction effect that threatened to sink rescue boats dispatched from the *Ile de France*, the *Stockholm,* and several other smaller ships that had converged at the disaster site. Waves also slammed rescue boats into the *Andrea Doria*'s side. It was not until 6 A.M., seven hours after the collision, that the last passenger was finally rescued. Four hours later, the totally capsized *Andrea Doria* sank 240 feet to the ocean floor. Only forty-six passengers died, most as a result of the initial collision.

Despite the fact that half the lifeboats were rendered useless, the rescue was successful for a number of reasons. An SOS alerted others to the disaster quickly. The ship managed to stay afloat for nearly eleven hours, allowing time for other ships to reach the scene. The collision occurred in a well-traveled sea corridor. The sailors from the rescue ships were willing to risk their lives, and those crew members who remained onboard the *Andrea Doria* were able to organize the passengers and help get them off the ship.

Rescue: So Close, So Far Away

The *Andrea Doria* was a successful at-sea rescue, but ships as diverse as the *Titanic* and the *Endurance,* lost in Antarctic ice in 1915, have foundered before help could arrive. Even the close proximity of rescuers is no guarantee that disaster can be averted. When the *Dona Paz* and the *Victor* collided in 1987, a great deal of oil was spilled and the ships caught on fire. The blaze spread to the water, making it impossible for nearby rescuers to approach.

Storms can also hinder rescue, as happened on October 23, 1918, when the Canadian *Princess Sophia* hit submerged rocks along the "inside passage" of Alaska's panhandle, from Skagway to Juneau. The *Sophia*'s captain decided to wait for high tide to maneuver his ship off the rocks, declining help from nearby rescue boats. Later that day, however, the storm

◄ The *Endurance* had to be abandoned by Ernest Shackleton and his fellow polar explorers when the ship became trapped in ice.

worsened and the rescue vessels had to retreat. Despite an urgent plea—"Taking water and foundering, for GOD's sake come and save us"[13]—from the *Sophia*'s captain, no vessels could approach during the storm. All 353 people onboard were killed.

Another major ship disaster in the United States, with massive loss of life, occurred while a ship was still tied to the dock on a river. This tragic incident took place in Chicago on July 24, 1915, a balmy Saturday. The Western Electric Company had hired six steamships for the annual company picnic and issued some seven thousand tickets to employees and their families. Many wanted to make the day cruise across the southern tip of Lake Michigan to Michigan City, Indiana, on the *Eastland,* one of the newer ships. It was scheduled to be the first of the six boats to leave the downtown Chicago River wharf. By 6:40 A.M., when the gangplanks were lowered, roughly five thousand people were waiting, most hoping to board the *Eastland.*

As people poured up the gangplank, the crowd's weight caused the ship—which was later determined to be top-heavy and unstable—to list toward the dock. The crew temporarily corrected the list by partially filling ballast tanks on the opposite, port (left) side of the ship. Within half an hour, the ship had taken on its capacity of twenty-five hundred passengers. As the crowd shifted to the other side of the ship for river views, the ship began to list to that side. The ballast tanks were emptied, and the ship momentarily leveled out once more, but the topsy-turvy vessel was not out of danger. The port list

MAROONED IN ANTARCTICA

One of the more spectacular tales of shipwreck and survival is that of the crew of the *Endurance.* British explorer Ernest Shackleton's goal was to sail the wooden-hulled ship from South Georgia, an island off the southern tip of South America, to the ice-covered continent of Antarctica. Shackleton would then lead the first expedition to cross Antarctica on foot. When Shackleton and his twenty-seven-man crew reached South Georgia in November 1914, however, they faced the worst ice conditions in living memory. Local whalers suggested they wait until next season, but it had been difficult to raise the money for the expedition, and in Europe, World War I was raging. To Shackleton it was now or never, and the ship began its trip into the Antarctic Circle in early December.

After wending its way through pack ice and ice floes for seven weeks, the *Endurance* became trapped as ice formed around it. Over the next eight months, the ice gradually tightened its grip. When the pressure of the ice knocked the *Endurance* on its side, the explorers were forced to abandon the ship that had been their home for nearly a year. They salvaged what they could and set up camp nearby. As the ice began to thaw, the *Endurance,* broken and battered, gradually began to sink beneath the ice. Finally, almost one year after the ship had set sail, it made its final plunge and disappeared.

Despite heavy odds against success, Shackleton and five others were eventually able to make a risky sea journey in a small boat back to South Georgia to seek help. On August 30, 1916, two years after the expedition's start, Shackleton and his comrades returned to rescue the marooned men. Not a single life was lost.

resumed at 7:20 A.M. and reached a critical point within ten minutes. Passengers and crew alike were slow to recognize the approaching disaster. At 7:30 the ship rolled onto its side.

▲ Survivors of the disastrous 1915 *Eastland* capsizing in the Chicago River file off the side of the ship and through the tug *Kenosha* to safety.

A Most Horrible Screaming

Passengers were thrown into the water; many people in those days did not know how to swim. Many more were trapped inside the ship. Rescue efforts began immediately, with some onlookers diving into the river to save lives. "I shall never be able to forget what I saw," one eyewitness said.

> People were struggling in the water, clustered so thickly that they literally covered the surface of the river. A few were swimming; the rest were floundering about, some clinging to a life raft that had floated free, others clutching at anything that they could reach—at bits of wood, at each other, grabbing each other, pulling each other down, and screaming! The screaming was the most horrible of all.[14]

With the ship on its side, rescuers cut holes in the hull to reach those trapped, and pleading for help, inside. Many of these victims drowned before they could be saved. By the end of the day, an appalling 844 men, women, and children had perished. Because the death toll included only two crew members and one rescuer, this was a higher number of passenger fatalities than the *Titanic*, which had suffered almost seven hundred crew deaths, three years earlier.

Improving Chances of Survival

Unless a ship goes down very close to shore, like the *Eastland*, the major challenge to saving people is finding them, and finding them fast. Historically, it could be months or even years before people on shore even knew that a ship had gone down. And although the Romans wrote regulations in 46 B.C. requiring assistance to shipwrecked seamen, it was not until the 1700s that organized efforts for saving sailors were begun

WIRELESS TO THE RESCUE

One of the most dramatic early cases of wireless to the rescue occurred on January 23, 1909. The *Florida*, an immigrant ship bound from Italy to New York, and the *Republic*, a palatial passenger liner carrying American tourists to Europe, collided in a dense fog fifty miles off the coast of Nantucket. Jack Binns, a twenty-six-year-old wireless operator on the badly damaged *Republic*, stayed at his post sending out a distress call. A nearby ship, the *Baltic*, responded and the more than sixteen hundred people onboard the *Republic* were transferred to it or the *Florida*, which remained seaworthy. (Five people died from the collision, which sank the *Republic*, making it the largest ship in the world to sink at that time.)

Binns was treated as a hero and brought to the nation's capital to testify before Congress. Unfortunately, lawmakers ignored his call for a federal law requiring full time wireless on ships. The successful *Republic* rescue also left shipbuilders feeling secure that wireless assured fast response in emergencies, and thus the need was for only enough lifeboats to ferry passengers from ship to ship, rather than enough lifeboats to hold all the passengers onboard. It was not until three years later, in the aftermath of the *Titanic* tragedy, that Congress passed legislation requiring all transatlantic ships to have a wireless operator on duty twenty-four hours a day.

to be put into effect. The Chinese offered money and prizes for significant rescues. The British offered a reward to anyone who could figure out how to revive someone "near death" as the result of drowning or smoke inhalation.

In the United States, the Massachusetts Humane Society spearheaded efforts to help shipwreck survivors. In 1807 the society built refuge huts along the sparsely populated coastline to provide shelter for survivors. By the end of the century, the huts were equipped with boats and other equipment, and a volunteer lifesaving service was put in place. But only those who were shipwrecked on sandbars and reefs close to shore stood a chance of being rescued.

Today, although it is possible for a ship to go down so suddenly that there is no time to send out a distress signal, in most cases an SOS is issued. The primitive, low-power wireless transmitter onboard the *Titanic*, which had a guaranteed range of 250 miles, has been replaced by sophisticated satellite-based global communications and locating systems.

From Life Rings to EPIRBs

Safety regulations and technological advances have also vastly improved the chances of surviving a shipwreck. Conventional safety equipment—the life ring for a person overboard, life jackets, lifeboats, flares and rockets, air horns, strobe lights, and smoke canisters—has been supplemented with innovative emergency gear. For example, open-sea immersion suits covering all but the face are capable of preserving body heat for precious extra hours. (Immersion suits are also known as survival suits, though survival is hardly guaranteed.) Life rafts may be stocked with radios, water purifiers, and other crucial survival equipment.

High-tech directional devices are another essential component for passenger safety. In the United States, commercial vessels today are required to have an Emergency Position Indicating Radio Beacon (EPIRB). The latest EPIRBs are water-activated, so that if a ship capsizes or sinks, the device emits a satellite-detectable signal registered with the National Oceanic and Atmospheric Administration (NOAA). Within minutes of the device's being activated, NOAA and the Coast Guard know which vessel is in trouble and exactly where it is located.

▶ Maryland congressman Wayne Gilchrest, chairman of the Coast Guard and Maritime Transportation subcommittee, tests an immersion suit in Chesapeake Bay in April 2000.

Still, the difference between life and death often hangs on whether there is enough safety equipment, whether it is properly maintained and accessible, and whether the crew knows how to use it. On November 13, 1965, the *Yarmouth Castle*, an aging cruise ship with 550 passengers and crew onboard, left the port of Miami for a three-day cruise to the Bahamas. That night, at around 1 A.M., a cabin being used to store old mattresses, cans of paint, and other combustible materials, caught fire. The nearly forty-year-old ship had a steel hull but multiple wooden decks, wooden furniture, and highly flammable drapes and rugs. The *Yarmouth Castle* had also been painted many times, making it a virtual tinderbox. The cabin fire spread and the ship quickly became an inferno.

According to some reports, when the crew went to fight the fire, they found the fire hoses had been cut. Lifeboats, winches, even ropes had been painted, making them inoperable. No fire drills had been run, and the captain and some of the crew abandoned the ship in the first lifeboat, leaving the passengers to fend for themselves. (When this first lifeboat approached the *Finnpulp*, a Finnish freighter that had seen the fire and come to help, the *Finnpulp*'s captain frostily sent it back to help get the passengers off the burning ship.) The *Finnpulp* and another cruise ship managed to rescue 291 passengers and 174 crew members. Eighty-five passengers and two crew members died by the time the still-burning *Yarmouth Castle* sank around 6 A.M. The investigation that followed cited poor maintenance of rescue equipment, including the paint-blocked lifeboats and rafts; poorly trained crew members who knew nothing about the use of firefighting equipment; and the ship's hiring practices—to keep costs down, many of the crew spoke no English and had never been to sea.

◀ A survivor of the burning and sinking of the *Yarmouth Castle* stands wrapped in a blanket in front of the rescue ship *Bahama Star*.

Coast Guard Search and Rescue

In the United States, the Coast Guard, now part of the Homeland Security Department, is responsible for search-and-rescue missions. The agency maintains search-and-rescue facilities on the East, West, and Gulf Coasts; in Alaska, Hawaii, Guam, and Puerto Rico; and on the Great Lakes and inland waterways. When alerted to an emergency, Coast Guard technicians pinpoint the location of the ship and feed information

▼ Rescuers pull an African refugee from the water off the coast of Spain after his makeshift boat sank.

on currents and wind conditions into their computers. This helps rescuers in locating possible survivors.

Search-and-rescue coordination centers quickly dispatch small planes, helicopters, and boats to locate and rescue sailors in distress. Because search-and-rescue missions often take place under the worst conditions possible (at night, in fierce weather and raging seas), the Coast Guard has acquired more than eighty specially designed "motor lifeboats." The newest such boats are forty-seven feet long and have technologies that make them almost unsinkable. For example, they are self-bailing and self-righting, capable of returning to an upright position within eight seconds if overturned.

The Coast Guard also has an elite corps of helicopter-based rescue swimmers, who are often called upon to work during thunderstorms, snow, high winds, heavy seas, and darkness. Rescue swimmers may be lowered by cable to a boat deck to stabilize and evacuate seriously injured people, or into the water to rescue people before they drown or die of hypothermia (a dangerous loss of body heat). Sometimes the rescue swimmer cannot be brought back up to the helicopter. When that happens the flight mechanic throws him or her an inflatable raft, which comes complete with an immersion suit, flashing light, and emergency position indicator beacon.

A Tragedy That Saved Lives

The Coast Guard says that during the decade after 1992, when the service began keeping formal records, rescue swimmers saved more than four thousand lives. The agency developed its corps of rescue swimmers in response to a maritime tragedy. On the evening of February 10, 1983, the *Marine Electric* left Norfolk, Virginia, to deliver twenty-five thousand tons of pulverized coal to Massachusetts. The wind was blowing at more than forty miles an hour, the sky was overcast, and the seas choppy, but the crew had worked through similar weather. The storm steadily worsened, however, and by the next morning the waves were up to forty feet high, and the wind was blowing at close to seventy miles per hour. The sea's pounding weakened rust spots on the ship's hatches, and water began pouring into the hold.

HYPOTHERMIA: THE SILENT KILLER

When a ship goes down, the difference between life and death frequently lies in the temperature of the water, since many shipwreck deaths are due to hypothermia rather than drowning. Hypothermia occurs when the body's core temperature drops to 95°F or below. Chances of survival are affected by how cold the water is—the colder the water, the quicker symptoms will develop. The body loses heat to water about thirty times faster than to air. The following chart, developed by the Mayo Clinic, summarizes the interplay of water temperature and exposure time as they affect how long a person can remain conscious, and then alive, in a body of water.

Water Temperature (in degrees F)	Time Until Exhaustion Or Unconsciousness	Expected Time of Survival in the Water
32.5	Less than 15 minutes	Less than 15–45 minutes
32.5–40	15–30 minutes	30–90 minutes
40–50	30–60 minutes	1–3 hours
50–60	1–2 hours	1–6 hours
60–70	2–7 hours	2–40 hours
70–80	3–12 hours	3 hours to indefinite
More than 80	Indefinite	Indefinite

A day and a half after leaving port, the captain sent out a distress call, and the Coast Guard responded immediately. But by the time a rescue helicopter reached the scene, the ship had sunk and the crew was in the water. The helicopter lowered rescue baskets but the frigid waters had taken their toll. Weakened by the effects of hypothermia, the men were unable to get themselves into the baskets. The helicopter pilot frantically called for a U.S. Navy chopper and rescue swimmer. The navy swimmer arrived on the scene two hours after the initial distress call, but for all but three of the thirty-four men it was too late.

Global maritime monitoring systems, rescue swimmers, EPIRBs, and all the rest have helped to address many crucial rescue issues today, and major reforms like mandating enough lifeboats for all passengers have increased survivability. Continued efforts at improving rescue are vital, however, because even the most advanced technology cannot prevent all accidents, and human error promises to be an ongoing factor in causing maritime catastrophes.

CHAPTER THREE

How Accidents Happen

A cts of war, equipment failures, and poor design have all been known to cause a shipwreck. Violent, stormy seas can batter almost any ship to oblivion. But the Coast Guard estimates that well over half of all reported maritime accidents involve errors of seamanship or navigation. Seamanship errors include things like the person in charge not paying attention, being careless, reckless, or inexperienced, going too fast, or not posting a lookout. When factors that are not direct operator errors—inadequately maintained equipment, overloading a ship with cargo or with people, a poorly trained crew—combine with bad judgment, an accident at sea can seem almost inevitable.

Many accidents result from of a series of events—a chain of error—that leads up to a catastrophe. A fire that was caused by a carelessly tossed match and that should be easily extinguished, for example, blazes freely because the firefighting equipment is not accessible, or because the crew does not know how to use it. A collision damages a ship, but it would have stayed afloat if the portholes in passenger cabins were not open, allowing even more water to pour in and destabilize the vessel. Disaster expert James R. Chiles describes how the cruise ship *Royal Majesty* went aground near Nantucket in June 1995 after the cable to its global positioning system antenna came loose. He notes:

> Nobody on the ship's bridge noticed that the ship was miles off course. Normally the depth alarm would have gone off when less than ten feet of water remained under the hull, but somebody had set the alarm to stay quiet until zero feet of water remained. Such chains of error and mishap events occur throughout our modern world.[15]

Then again, there are those isolated incidents in which the gross incompetence and negligence of a single person can doom hundreds.

Wreck of the *Medusa*

Certainly one of the worst captains in history has to be Frenchman Hugues Duroy de Chaumereys, a former customs officer who was put in charge of a ship in 1816 based upon nothing more than his loyalty to King Louis XVIII. De Chaumereys had virtually no experience at sea when he took command of the *Medusa* for a voyage from France to Senegal, Africa. At sea, he ignored the advice of his well-trained crew, instead bowing to the wishes of a wealthy government official onboard who wanted to cut time off the trip by taking a dangerous coastal shortcut. To the further dismay of his crew, too lazy to plot his own course, de Chaumereys assigned navigational duties to a passenger with no prior experience. Inevitably, on a clear day, in calm water, the ship ran aground on a well-known and well-mapped sandbar off the coast of West Africa.

The captain's rescue plans were equally as self-serving and led to ruinous results. The ship had lifeboats for only about 250 of its 400 passengers. The lifeboats were loaded with the wealthiest passengers, provisions, navigational equipment, and the captain. A sixty-by-twenty-foot makeshift raft was built from ship timbers for the soldiers and crew, but it was so overcrowded with its 150 passengers that it mostly floated beneath the water's surface. Towing it proved difficult and, still four miles from land, the captain had the lifeboats cut it free. With no sails, oars, or compass, the raft was abandoned to the elements. Lacking provisions, scorched by the merciless sun during the day and frozen at night, the survivors on the raft turned vicious and desperate. Murder, suicide, and cannibalism quickly lightened the raft. "With unbearable thirst and hunger overcoming them, some of the men started tearing flesh from the corpses littering the raft. And one by one, soldiers and officers alike, consumed the dead," writes Alexander McKee in *Wreck of the Medusa: The Tragic Story of the Death Raft*.[16]

After twelve days adrift, a passing ship rescued a mere fifteen men left alive on the raft—and five of these died within weeks. The *Medusa*, when found nearly two months after

▲ Theodore Gericault's *The Raft of the Medusa* graphically captures the desperate situation these survivors faced after being abandoned at sea.

having been abandoned, still sat intact on the sandbar, home to three emaciated survivors out of seventeen who had refused to get on the death raft. The cavalier way that the captain and his cronies treated those abandoned on the raft scandalized the public and created a political uproar in France. De Chaumereys was court-martialed and tried for desertion but found not guilty. In 1819 the journey was immortalized in a dramatic painting by Theodore Gericault, *The Raft of the Medusa*, which hangs at the Louvre museum in Paris.

To Err Is Human

Human error can sometimes be of the monumental, de Chaumereys type, but more typically it runs the gamut from chronic incompetence to a single minor lapse in judgment that sparks off a disaster. Once again, the sinking of the *Titanic* serves as an excellent example of small mistakes that ultimately accumulated to become catastrophic. Binoculars that were supposed to be up in the crow's nest were missing, and no one on the bridge was willing to take the time to find another pair. As a result, the lookouts did not see the iceberg until it was almost upon them. Captain Smith had sailed for forty years without ever being involved in a serious accident, and so may have grown complacent, and possibly even reckless. Despite knowing that he was approaching an ice field, he failed to post extra lookouts, he did not reduce the ship's speed, and he passed only one wireless message warning of ice to his bridge officers.

Mental shock may also have greatly contributed to the scope of the *Titanic* disaster. Although Smith learned almost immediately that the ship was going to sink, he failed to tell his officers and crew, delaying the launching of lifeboats and leaving many seats empty when the first few did leave. Surviving crew members reported that Smith seemed unable to respond to the emergency once he realized that the ship was doomed and many people were going to lose their lives. Daniel Allen Butler writes of Smith in *"Unsinkable": The Full Story of RMS Titanic*:

> Just about midnight, his powers of decision and command seemed to desert him. For the next two hours and twenty minutes, he would be only a shadow of his former self,

▼ *Titanic* captain Edward Smith, right, with purser Herbert McElroy, committed a number of mistakes that ultimately cost many lives.

AN ACCIDENT WAITING TO HAPPEN

Human error, poor judgment, and business policies that turned a blind eye to sloppy operational procedures were all in play when the *Exxon Valdez* ran aground in 1989. The vessel was seriously undermanned—to save money, Exxon had reduced the crew from twenty-four to fourteen, leaving the men tired and overworked. Neither the captain nor any other licensed watch officer paced the bridge at the time of the accident. The pilot navigating the ship was not licensed to operate in Prince William Sound and the navigation school he "graduated" from was a home study program. The helmsman on duty had been reported as incompetent in the past.

The Alaska Oil Spill Commission's "Case Study of the *Exxon Valdez* Oil Spill" summed it up nicely: "The grounding of the *Exxon Valdez* was not an isolated, freak occurrence. It was simply one result of policies, habits, and practices that for nearly two decades have infused the nation's maritime oil transportation system with increasing levels of risk. The *Exxon Valdez* was an accident waiting to happen."

isolating himself on the bridge, failing to pass on critical information to his officers and senior seamen, acting and reacting slowly to reports and rapidly changing circumstances, and giving half-hearted orders, some of which the crew would openly defy.[17]

The competency and mental state of a ship captain has great importance because of the marine tradition that a captain's command over his or her vessel is virtually absolute. First mates and other sailors lower down the chain of authority often defer unquestioningly to the captain. "With so much riding on one person," says Perrow, "it is not surprising that many of the worst marine disasters stem from incompetent captains."[18]

An Assassin's Knife at Sea

Perrow also notes that the authority invested in captains hits a major snag when two ships are in danger of colliding. Not accustomed to relinquishing authority, the captains often refuse to cooperate, with disastrous results. The situation is worsened as the world's waterways become ever more crowded with tankers, cruise ships, and pleasure boats. Miscommunication between the two vessels is often compounded by over-reliance on technology or a simple lack of attention.

Collisions sometimes occur, as between the *Andrea Doria* and *Stockholm*, out in the open ocean, but they are even more of a concern in the confined spaces of rivers, harbors, and straits. One of North America's worst shipwrecks, on May 29, 1914, was due to a collision in the St. Lawrence River, near Quebec City. The Canadian Pacific passenger ship *Empress of Ireland*, carrying 1,477 people, and the Norwegian coal ship *Storstad* initially spotted one another around 2 A.M. They were still six miles apart, the liner heading north to begin a transatlantic journey to Liverpool and the collier approaching its offloading destination of Montreal. As they began to close on each other, a thick fog rolled in, reducing visibility to zero. The rules of the sea call for ships meeting head-on to turn to starboard and pass each other port-to-port, but to maintain direction if on a starboard-to-starboard course. In the night fog, the *Empress of Ireland* gave three short whistle blasts, signaling its intention to come to a stop. Unfortunately, the *Storstad* had taken a course to pass port-to-port. Despite trading a series of warning whistles, at 1:55 A.M. the *Storstad* barreled out of the fog headed directly for the stationary *Empress of Ireland*. *Storstad*'s reinforced bow, designed for cutting through pack ice in Scandinavian waters, plunged "between the liner's steel ribs as smoothly as an assassin's knife,"[19] declared British journalist James Croall. The devastating collision left a hole fourteen feet wide and twenty-five feet high in the *Empress of Ireland*.

A Final Fourteen Minutes

The *Empress* had plenty of life vests and lifeboats onboard, the crew was highly trained, and the ship was built for safety. But within a minute, the *Empress of Ireland* was listing nine degrees. The ship was designed to sustain the type of damage caused by the collision. In addition to the hull breach, however, portholes left open by passengers who wanted air were allowing water to pour into the ship at an accelerated pace. Open portholes were strictly against regulations, but it was a rule frequently broken, especially on sheltered rivers like the St. Lawrence.

Many of the passengers were asleep at the time of the collision, and woke to find themselves trapped in rapidly flooding cabins. As the ship continued to roll to its side, close to seven hundred men, women, and children climbed over the rail onto the ship's side. Shockingly, a mere fourteen minutes

▲ One of the thousand-plus victims of the *Empress of Ireland* disaster is brought ashore in Quebec.

after the collision, the ship made her final roll and sank. There had been time for only one SOS to be sent, and only seven lifeboats were launched. Most of the 465 people who survived were first class passengers whose cabins were on higher decks, enabling them to reach the lifeboats quickly. It was nearly two hours before rescue ships reached the scene. By then 1,012 people had either succumbed to hypothermia or drowned.

Maritime experts have noted that the collision would not have occurred if both ships had just maintained their initial headings. Also, the heavy fog should have prompted the *Storstad* to slow. The *Empress of Ireland* captain was faulted for failing to close his ship's watertight doors as a precautionary measure before the collision.

Crowded Ports

Despite advances in radar and communications technology, collisions still occur today, even in shipping lanes where traffic is monitored very closely. A typical example of ship-to-ship and ship-to-shore miscommunication occurred on August 10, 1993, when three vessels under the control of harbor pilots collided in Florida's Tampa Bay. (Pilots temporarily come onboard ships in harbors to help dock them and steer them through busy channels.)

Early in the morning of that day, the freighter *Balsa 37* was making her way out of the harbor as the combined tug and barge *Seafarer* was coming in to dock. The two ships collided at the intersection of two channels, causing a fire and explosion aboard the *Seafarer*. To minimize the impact of the collision, the *Balsa 37* veered away and collided with the tug/barge *Captain Fred Bouchard*, rupturing a cargo tank. An estimated 336,000 gallons of fuel oil were dumped into Tampa Bay. Oil cleanup alone cost $25 million. An investigation by the National Transportation Safety Board found that, although the pilots of the three vessels had been in communication, they had not supplied one another with all the pertinent information.

The pilot aboard the *Balsa 37* did not know that the *Seafarer* and the *Bouchard* had made an overtaking agreement between themselves. That overtaking agreement meant the *Balsa* would pass the other two side-by-side in a bend, rather than in tandem as the *Balsa* pilot expected. Several possible reasons

▼ Miscommunication led to one of the two barges involved in a three-ship collision in Tampa Bay sustaining heavy damage.

DANGER FROM BELOW

In most collisions, a captain sees what he or she is about to collide with, even if it is at the last minute. The twentieth century introduced a new hazard: collisions between surface ships and submarines. On February 9, 2001, the crew of the *Greeneville*, a nuclear-powered submarine, was demonstrating the ship's maneuvering capabilities for civilian guests onboard. To the Japa-nese fishermen on the *Ehime Maru*, it must have seemed as if old legends of sea monsters had come true when the sub, making a rapid ascent from a depth of about four hundred feet, surfaced suddenly, ripping through the bottom of their boat. Nine of the thirty-five persons aboard the Japanese vessel, which sank after the collision, died.

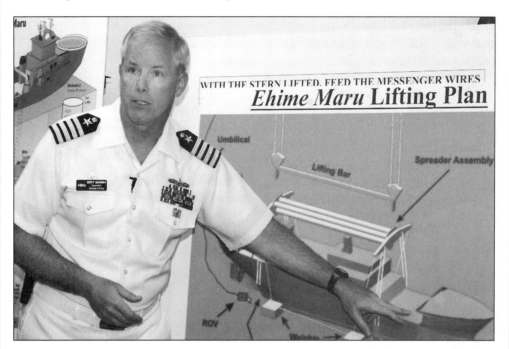

▲ In August 2001 a U.S. Navy official shows how the service hopes to retrieve the *Ehime Maru* from the floor of the Pacific, off the coast of Hawaii in order to recover the remains of the nine victims.

for the *Balsa* pilot's lack of understanding of the impending two-abreast passing were cited. He may not have heard the agreement being made, possibly because he was distracted by other business. The pilot also apparently did not use the ship's radar to monitor the approaching vessels, and he did not recognize what was happening by observing the approaching vessels' running lights in the early morning darkness.

The "*Titanic* of the Mississippi"

Design flaws and shoddy construction have been factors contributing to shipwrecks through the ages. In the early days of shipbuilding, engineering principles were not well understood. Ship owners wanted vessels designed to carry larger cargoes or more passengers. Some of these changes made the ships top-heavy, difficult to maneuver, and extremely vulnerable in rough seas and stormy weather. As ships converted from sail to steam, tens of thousands of lives were lost before the new technology was completely mastered. In the United States, in the single year of 1823, ship boiler explosions killed more than a thousand people. Steamboats on the Mississippi River had an average life span of about five years before they burned, crashed, or sank.

One of the most tragic disasters of the nineteenth century was triggered by a combination of design flaw, imperfect technology, and human greed. Because it occurred on the Mississippi River, it is often called the "*Titanic* of the Mississippi." At the end of the Civil War, thousands of Union soldiers

▼ *Harper's Weekly* used this wood engraving in 1865 to illustrate the catastrophic explosion and fire onboard the *Sultana.*

EXPLOSION OF THE STEAMER "SULTANA," April 28, 1865.

A FATAL FLAW

The *Kronan*, one of the most famous ships in Swedish history, sank as a result of design miscalculations. The largest and most powerful warship of its time, the *Kronan* led the Swedes into the Battle of Ôland against Danish and Dutch ships on June 1, 1676. The *Kronan* was reportedly a magnificent fighting ship, but it had not been designed to carry the extremely heavy cannons and other armament placed on her decks. Stabil-ity testing at the time, moreover, was somewhat unscientific—thirty sailors or so would be gathered to quickly run from one side of the ship to the other. Under full sail in a gusting wind, the dangerously top-heavy battleship turned too fast, heeled, capsized, exploded, and sank, taking eight hundred men to their deaths. The loss was a national disaster for Sweden, costing the country control of the southern Baltic.

who had been held in hellish Confederate prisoner-of-war camps anxiously waited to return home, and the federal government was paying steamboat operators five dollars a head to transport them up the river. J. Cass Mason, captain of the steamboat *Sultana*, was determined to cash in on this bonanza and make as big a profit as possible.

Although a crack had developed in one of the *Sultana*'s boilers, when the ship pulled up to the dock in Vicksburg, Mississippi, on April 24, 1865, Mason convinced the boiler-maker to put a temporary patch on it. The *Sultana* had four iron boilers that lay close together, lined up in a row. If one boiler had a problem, all of them were likely to be affected. But Mason downplayed the danger and promised that he would return later for a full overhaul.

After the repair at least twenty-three hundred people were loaded on the steamboat, which had a legal carrying capacity of fewer than five hundred people. At 2 A.M. on the morning of April 27, three of the *Sultana*'s boilers exploded. Decks collapsed, trapping some passengers; within twenty minutes the boat was engulfed in flames. An estimated eighteen hundred people died that night.

Roll On, Float Off

Ship engines no longer explode with regularity but other design problems continue to plague modern vessels. The inherent weakness in how roll-on/roll-off ferries are designed, for example, has been responsible for a number of disasters. The huge, close-to-water-level doors in these ships save ferry companies much time and money, compared to hauling autos onboard with a crane, for example. But any mechanical or human error that allows these doors to open at sea potentially exposes the entire inside hull. This can lead to a disastrous inrush of water that can sink a ferry in minutes.

The Swedish-owned *Estonia*, a ro-ro car and passenger ferry, sank on September 28, 1994, in the Baltic Sea, claiming as many as 850 lives. It was a stormy night, and the battering by extremely rough seas tripped the locking device of the gate on the vehicle deck. Water poured in quickly, swamping the deck. The ferry capsized and sank in minutes, trapping most passengers inside. The investigation found that the locking mechanism had also failed on other ships, but that the systematic collection and analysis of data that would have identified the design flaw and alerted others had not occurred.

While the design flaw may have been the direct cause of the *Estonia* sinking, human error played a part in magnifying the tragedy. The bridge officers were not watching the television monitors that would have told them they were taking on water, nor did they communicate with the control room to determine where the water was coming from once it was discovered. As a result, they did not slow the speed of the boat, which contributed significantly to how quickly it capsized. In addition, the passengers were not informed of the problem until too late and inadequate rescue forces were called in. Only 150 people survived.

A Trial-and-Error Process

In other cases, the process of converting a boat from one purpose to another can compromise a design that was initially fine. Conversion, which refers to changing a boat's design to accommodate new tasks or equipment, has been the cause of a number of losses suffered by the commercial fishing industry. The naval architect John Womack explains:

> Commercial fishing boat design in the U.S. has a history of being a trial and error process of development for many of the fisheries. Many fishing boats, though originally safe when designed and built by a qualified designer and yard, are modified by their crews as fishing methods change or the boat changes fisheries. These modifications are made many times without checking their effect on a boat's stability.[20]

The modifications almost always decrease a boat's stability, making it more likely a boat will capsize, particularly when overloaded or in heavy seas. One of the contributing factors to the sinking of the *Andrea Gail*, described in the book *The Perfect Storm* by Sebastian Junger, was the boat's instability as a result of conversion.

"Fire! Fire!"

Fire at sea has been a major concern since the days of wind and oar power. Design flaws, poor maintenance practices, and human error can all cause fires onboard ships. Simple carelessness could be especially lethal prior to about the middle of the nineteenth century, when ships were built of wood and powered by cloth sails. The sailing ship *Fame* caught fire in 1824, during a voyage from Sumatra to England, when a crew member drained brandy from a cask using a candle for light. The entire ship was engulfed in flames within twenty minutes. Although the property loss was great, nobody died.

Soon ships were being built of iron, and eventually steel, and powered by steam engines. Steam engines meant trips could be made more quickly, and storms could be avoided more easily because the ships no longer were dependent on the wind. But steam engines, powered by huge boilers, were notoriously temperamental and exploded frequently, as happened to the *Sultana*. Furthermore, the new shipbuilding technologies developed between 1850 and 1900 allowed passenger ships to almost triple in size, magnifying the potential for large-scale disasters.

On June 15, 1904, a ship fire caused one of the worst disasters in New York City's history. On that day more than thirteen hundred German immigrants from a single neighborhood, most of them women and children, boarded the *General Slocum* to go on a church picnic up the East River. As the ship was underway, someone tossed a match into an illegally stored barrel of hay. The boat, a paddlewheel-powered excursion ferry built in 1891, had been painted multiple times and was a firetrap. "It was only a matter of seconds until the entire forward part of the boat was a mass of flames," the *New York Times* reported. "All this time full speed ahead was maintained, and the flames, fanned fiercely by the wind, ate their way swiftly toward the hapless women and babies that were crowded on all the decks astern." From his pilothouse the ship's captain viewed "a fierce blaze—the wildest I have ever seen."[21]

THE BURNING OF THE *MORRO CASTLE*

Aging ships, poorly maintained fire-fighting equipment, and badly trained crews almost guarantee that if a fire does start, it will be difficult to contain. One of the early cruise liners, the *Morro Castle*, managed to combine almost all of these factors. On September 8, 1934, three days after the ship left Havana, Cuba, for New York City, a fire of suspicious origin was discovered at 2:45 A.M. in one of the public rooms on the promenade deck. The room, full of wood furniture and paneling and layers of highly flammable paint, was quickly an inferno. Firefighting efforts were impeded by the fact that fire hoses had been removed and, because passengers had been playing with the hoses on a previous trip, fire hydrants in passenger areas were capped. The fire detection system had been altered from its original design and was not working. The ship's captain did not respond quickly to the crisis, nor did he allocate enough men to fight the blaze initially. It spread rapidly, whipped by high winds. Panicking passengers began jumping ship. Several lifeboats, also painted multiple times, burned in place. Only a few lifeboats were released. During the night 134 people died. A later investigation found the crew to be poorly trained in firefighting and emergency procedures.

▲ A still-smoking *Morro Castle* is beached at Asbury Park, New Jersey, on the day after its fatal fire.

People leapt from the ship, their clothes aflame, but few could swim and the currents were strong. More than one thousand people died. The captain, first mate, officers of the steamboat company, and a steamboat inspector were indicted as the inquiry heard evidence of rotted fire hoses, disintegrating life jackets, and an inexperienced crew. Only the captain was convicted, for not holding fire drills, not training the crew properly, and not maintaining fire apparatus.

▶ Firefighting tugboats were called in to battle the blaze in the aft section of the cruise ship *Ecstasy*.

An Ongoing Concern

Today fire remains one of the biggest concerns of the cruise ship industry. Modern cruise ships have a lot of flammable material, and every passenger who smokes is a potential accident waiting to happen. From 1979 to 1999, sixteen of the twenty-five major accidents involving foreign cruise ships operating from U.S. ports involved fires. Not all involved loss of life, but the potential for tragedy can be huge.

This was memorably demonstrated on July 20, 1998, when the lives of thirty-five hundred people were endangered by a fire on the cruise ship *Ecstasy*. The ship was carrying 2,565 passengers and 916 crew members on a run from Miami to Key West, Florida. The fire started when crew members performed unauthorized welding in the main laundry, igniting a large accumulation of lint in the ventilation system. The fire moved through the ventilation system, creating intense heat and smoke. The ship ultimately lost power and steering and began to drift. The fire, caused by inadequately maintained equipment and human carelessness, caused an estimated $17 million in damages. Fortunately, no one was killed, although one passenger needed to be hospitalized.

According to the subsequent National Transportation Safety Board investigation, the fact that the *Ecstasy* did not have an automatic fire suppression system on the mooring deck contributed to the extensive fire damage. The board issued a number of recommendations to *Ecstasy* owner Carnival as well as to other cruise line companies, including that they immediately inspect their ships' laundry ventilation systems for combustible materials. The board also restated its call for the installation of automatic local-sounding smoke alarms in passenger and crew accommodation areas, so that everyone onboard a ship receives immediate warning of a possible fire and thus has the maximum available time to escape.

The More Things Change . . .

According to marine accident investigator K.M. Varghese, in the sixteenth century, anyone taking a long voyage on a ship had perhaps a 50 percent chance of arriving safely. He notes that in 1822, an English newspaper determined that two thousand vessels and twenty thousand people had perished at sea throughout Europe during the winter of 1821. A study investigating the high loss of life in shipwrecks, conducted a few years later by the English House of Commons, found that the most common causes included defective construction of ships, inadequate equipment, imperfect state of repairs, improper and excessive loading, incompetence of masters and officers, drunkenness, and imperfect charts.

The annual loss of life in marine accidents worldwide has been reduced but, Varghese says, "We have the same problems today."[22] He goes on to note that, as a byproduct of British lawmakers' concern for identifying the causes of shipwrecks, the first systematic attempts were undertaken to investigate marine accidents. Nowadays, disaster-at-sea investigations are even more important, and more challenging to conduct.

Investigations at Sea

U p until fairly recently, shipwrecks were routinely blamed on storms or on the actions of the captain and crew. Today, regardless of whether the accident involves a grounding, collision, fire, or spill, investigators focus on both the immediate cause of an accident, and any underlying factors. In a recent report to the British government, retired admiral John S. Lang, chief inspector of marine accidents for the United Kingdom, summed up an investigator's role:

> In the past many casualties were, in most people's minds, caused by a single event, often described as human error. This was a convenient means of concluding an investigation; and it was all too easy to blame one person for whatever happened. Many companies did no more than dismiss the unfortunate individual and felt they had dealt with the problem satisfactorily. But no accident is ever caused by a single action. Each one is a combination of circumstances that come together to cause the event and it is essential that both the initiating and underlying causes are identified to prevent the same thing happening again. It falls to the marine accident investigator to identify the component parts of this causal chain and to explain what happened with a view to prevent it happening again.[23]

The primary goal of modern shipwreck investigators is to establish the facts of what happened in order to prevent future accidents and to improve safety measures. At the same time much can be learned from investigations of high-profile disasters like the *Lusitania*, the *Titanic*, and the *Maine*. The original investigations as well as subsequent ones carried out in the ensuing decades can offer important insights into personalities, technology, and institutions. Interest remains high because of such shipwrecks' historical significance, and as technology becomes more sophisticated, and old records become available, new insights are likely to be gained.

The *Lusitania*'s Final Crossing

The sinking of the *Lusitania* by a German submarine at the beginning of World War I is one of the most controversial wartime attacks on a civilian ship in history. The *Lusitania* was a luxury passenger liner described by its owners as a floating palace. With its powerful engines it had broken speed records for crossing the Atlantic. On May 1, 1915, the United States was not yet involved in the war when the *Lusitania*, sailing under a British flag, left New York for Liverpool, England. That very morning, the Imperial German Embassy had placed a framed "Notice!" in New York newspapers, as well as signs along Manhattan piers, reminding travelers that Germany and Great Britain were at war. The notice warned

▼ The *New York Times*'s headline coverage of the *Lusitania* sinking was more restrained than many British newspapers'; inset is the notice that the German Embassy had placed in the *Times* before the *Lusitania*'s final voyage.

that "vessels flying the flag of Great Britain, or any of her allies, are liable to destruction."[24] Evidently few people heeded the warning, as the *Lusitania* left port carrying 1,962 passengers and crew.

Early in the afternoon a week later, as the *Lusitania* approached the coast of southern Ireland, the German sub *U-20* torpedoed the liner. One passenger said the torpedo impact sounded like a "million-ton hammer hitting a steel boiler, a hundred feet high and a hundred yards in length." A second massive explosion occurred immediately after the first, "the expansion of which lifted the bows of the ship out of the water."[25]

The ship sank so fast that no more than a few lifeboats could be launched. Panicked passengers scrambled to find life preservers. The ship's crew had not run any fire or emergency drills, which was typical for that era. As a result, many passengers put the newly redesigned life jackets on upside down. Upon jumping into the water, many of these passengers flipped head down and drowned. Many others entered the water without life jackets. Even those who had found a life jacket and donned it correctly had just a small chance of surviving. The water temperature was 52°F; most would lose consciousness within an hour or two from hypothermia. Death was not far behind. By the time rescue boats arrived at about 6 P.M., the disaster had claimed the lives of 1,201 people, including 128 Americans.

The attack on an apparently unarmed passenger ship carrying innocent civilians provoked worldwide outrage. "The reaction in the British press," Diana Preston notes in her authoritative *Lusitania: An Epic Tragedy*, "was bitter, virulent, and predictable. The papers raged about the 'Latest Achievements of German Frightfulness at Sea' and 'The Hun's Most Ghastly Crime.'"[26] Media and government figures in other countries spoke of the attack as an act of unprecedented atrocity. Germany was surprised by the worldwide condemnation. German newspapers portrayed the *Lusitania* as a legitimate target of war, celebrated the sinking as "an extraordinary success,"[27] and accused Britain of using "citizens from neutral nations as a shield."[28]

Crime or Conspiracy?

Investigations at the time of the sinking were colored by wartime politics, and it would take decades to uncover the full facts and establish fault in the incident. The first inquiry into

REMEMBER THE *MAINE*!

Much of what happened to the *Lusitania* seemed to repeat the history of another famous ship, the *Maine*, sunk under controversial circumstances during wartime. In the late 1890s, while Cuban guerrillas were fighting Spain for independence, President William McKinley sent the *Maine* to anchor in Havana harbor as a show of support for Cuba and to protect American interests. On February 15, 1898, a massive explosion erupted through the battleship's hull, killing 266 of 354 soldiers onboard. American newspapers blamed Spain for the attack and whipped up war fever. Several weeks later, in April, the United States declared war on Spain, which American forces won in a matter of months.

"The cause of the explosion has been a mystery for a century," writer Thomas B. Allen noted in *National Geographic*. "In 1898 a U.S. Navy court of inquiry ruled that a large mine blew up beneath the ship. A second investigation in 1911 blamed a smaller mine farther aft. But an authoritative report in 1976, sponsored by Adm. Hyman G. Rickover, declared that the blast had been an accident probably started by a fire in a coal bunker." A detailed study in 1998 using computer modeling and simulations, sponsored by the National Geographic Society, determined that the evidence remains inconclusive, and the cause of the explosion remains unknown.

▲ Twelve years after the controversial sinking, observers in a small boat inspect wreckage from the *Maine* in Havana harbor.

SHOWING GUNS SHE DID *NOT* CARRY! A GERMAN FICTION-PICTURE OF THE SINKING OF THE "ENGLISH AUXILIARY-CRUISER 'LUSITANIA.'"

This German picture of the sinking of the "English Auxiliary-Cruiser 'Lusitania'" (Hilfskreuzer), is designed with deliberate malice to perpetuate the German official false statement that the "Lusitania" carried guns. Two quick-firers behind armoured-shields are shown on the upper deck forward, on either side of the forecastle near the bows. Apart from official contradictions by the Captain and owners of the "Lusitania."—President Wilson, in his second Note to the Berlin Government of June 11, declared explicitly that the "Lusitania" "was not armed for offensive action. . . . The Imperial German Government has been misinformed." Since then Stahl, the German secret-service agent in New York, who swore that he "saw guns on board the 'Lusitania,'" has been arrested on "the charge of perjury."

the sinking of the *Lusitania* was conducted by John J. Horgan, the coroner for County Kinsale, Ireland, where the survivors and the bodies of the dead were brought. His verdict: The government of Germany was guilty of the "appalling crime" of "wilful and wholesale murder."[29] An investigative inquiry led by Lord Mersey in Great Britain several months later concurred, finding that the German sub had fired two torpedoes. An investigation in the United States in 1918 absolved the *Lusitania*'s captain, William Turner, and shipping-line owner Cunard of all blame. It agreed with Mersey's conclusion that there had been two torpedoes, and called the sinking an illegal act by the German government.

Germany maintained that the *Lusitania* was carrying war materiél and Canadian troops, making her a legitimate military target. The U-boat commander's log (daily record) indicated that just one torpedo was fired. Germany claimed that the second, larger explosion that had occurred was proof that the *Lusitania* was carrying explosives to the war front. A German propaganda illustration even showed guns on the deck of the sinking *Lusitania*. The German government went on to accuse the British Admiralty (the navy's top

▲ A caption on this "German fiction-picture" of the *Lusitania* sinking says that it shows guns "she did *not* carry!"

executive authorities) of concealing evidence, engaging in conspiracy, and intentionally endangering noncombatants in order to push the United States into the war. Although the United States did not enter into World War I until nearly two years later, in April 1917, the sinking of the *Lusitania* is credited with nudging the country closer to war. Once engaged, "Remember the *Lusitania!*" became a battle cry among U.S. soldiers.

Questions festered for decades: Was the *Lusitania* secretly carrying armaments? What caused the second explosion? Was there a conspiracy among government officials in Great Britain to allow the Germans to sink the ship in hopes of dragging the United States into the war?

New Findings Cloud the Water

Over the years, multiple *Lusitania* investigations have been carried out, and the evolution of high-tech diving tools has shed new light on the question of what happened that fateful day. Written documents that have become available with the passage of time show that British naval authorities knew that Germany considered the *Lusitania* a legitimate target and was hoping to sink her. The Admiralty sent several very general messages to the *Lusitania* to alert the crew that submarines were patrolling the area, but other than that did very little to protect her. When the initial inquiries were held, the British Admiralty knew from messages that had been intercepted and decoded that only one torpedo had been fired.

The information was suppressed, however, because both British and U.S. officials were concerned about what had caused the second explosion. They knew the ship was in fact carrying illegal war materiél, and that public opinion would have shifted sharply if the ship's manifest, which listed forty-two hundred cases of rifle ammunition, 12,500 cases of shrapnel, and eighteen boxes of percussion fuses, had become widely known. Internal memos prepared by Admiralty staff show a clear desire to blame the loss of the ship solely on Captain Turner.

Famed *Titanic* investigator Robert Ballard led an expedition in 1993 to explore the *Lusitania* wreck to try to determine what caused the second explosion: illegal armaments, or something else. His team deployed a mini yellow submarine and two robotic undersea vehicles to photograph the wreck, which rests 270 feet below the surface. Ballard did not find a hole in the cargo hold, disproving the second torpedo theory. He speculates that the torpedo fired by the *U-20* may have hit next to an empty coal bunker, kicking up a lot of dust. Coal dust combined with oxygen is as explosive as dynamite. It is possible that a spark from the initial explosion was enough to detonate a second explosion.

These modern findings alter the historical perspective, suggesting that the *Lusitania*'s captain, the Cunard Line, and the British Admiralty bore some responsibility for the tragedy. They also serve as a prime example of some of the political as well as physical challenges marine investigators face when a well-known ship goes down.

Diagnosing "the Disease of Sloppiness"

The response to the sinking of the *Herald of Free Enterprise* demonstrates the wide variety of factors that may come into play in a modern marine accident investigation. On March 6, 1987, the *Herald*, a state-of-the-art roll-on/roll-off vehicle and passenger ferry, began to take on water within ninety seconds of leaving port in Zeebrugge, Belgium, on a trip to cross the

▼ The Townsend Thoresen ferry *Herald of Free Enterprise* accident might have claimed more lives if it had happened in deeper water.

English Channel to Dover, England. She quickly rolled onto her side, resting half-submerged on a sandbar in shallow water. Some 193 passengers and crew lost their lives, making this the most disastrous peacetime sinking of a British ship since the loss of the *Titanic*. Many others among the 539 people onboard were injured, and the death toll likely would have been higher if the boat had not settled on the sandbar rather than in deeper water nearby.

The immediate cause of the disaster was apparent even during the rescue: The ferry had left the dock with its bow door open, and the lower decks were almost immediately swamped. Interviews with survivors established how this seemingly unthinkable oversight happened—the crew member who was supposed to close the doors went off-duty to get some sleep, and the ship's design made it impossible for the captain on the bridge to see that the door had been left open during departure from the dock. The official inquiry concluded that serious errors were made by the crew. But the investigators also questioned executives from Townsend Thoreson, which owned and operated the ferry, and delved into the company's overall safety policy, management, and oversight. The accident report concluded:

> A full investigation into the circumstances of the disaster leads inexorably to the conclusion that the underlying or cardinal faults lay higher up in the Company [that owned the ship] . . . . From top to bottom the body corporate was infected with the disease of sloppiness . . . . The failure on the part of the shore management to give proper and clear directions was a contributory cause of the disaster [and] reveals a staggering complacency.[30]

Who Has Jurisdiction?

Because shipping is truly a global industry, one of the first issues modern shipwreck investigations face is simply "Who's in charge?" What happens when a collision occurs out in the middle of the ocean? Or when two ships from different countries collide in the waters of a third country? The International Maritime Organization (IMO), a specialized agency established by the United Nations in 1948, is responsible for developing and overseeing the laws and regulations that govern global shipping. Several international treaties require countries to conduct an inquiry into serious accidents that involve a ship they have registered. But the IMO has no enforcement authority and can only "invite" nations to investigate accidents, or to cooperate with other countries in an investigation.

In practice, lack of cooperation between countries is frequently a problem. Only a few countries, such as Finland, the Netherlands, Sweden, Australia, the United Kingdom, and the United States, have permanent professional investigative teams that are wholly independent. Elsewhere, the same people who investigate an accident are also responsible for

SAME ACCIDENT, DIFFERENT CONCLUSIONS

The question of jurisdiction and conflicting interests is not a new problem. When the British-registered *Empress of Ireland* and the Norwegian *Storstad* collided in the St. Lawrence River in 1914, two inquiries were held. The British inquiry convened in Quebec City determined that the accident was the fault of the chief officer of the Norwegian ship. The Norwegian inquiry found the crew of *Storstad* free of blame and concluded that the captain of the *Empress* had violated protocol by not passing port-to-port.

▲ *Empress of Ireland* captain Henry Kendall, facing left, testifies at the British inquiry into the sinking.

inspecting ships, or drawing up and enforcing the regulations. This can often lead to conflicts of interest. In still other countries, no single government agency or department has a clear mandate to investigate marine accidents, which can lead to bureaucratic infighting, or to no investigation at all.

Even when the countries do cooperate, there can be difficulties. When the ferry *Estonia* sank off Finland's coast in 1994, a three-country investigative commission was formed. An official report issued in 1997 concluded that a design flaw in the ship's bow door caused the disaster. The investigation was fraught with controversy, however, and the commission was accused of suppressing and manipulating evidence.

Lawyers for the German company that built the ferry called the report "worth less than the paper it is written on."[31] The company formed an independent "Group of Experts" that issued a report in 2000, concluding that the *Estonia* was unseaworthy when she left port due to reckless operation, poor maintenance, and careless inspections. A third group, the London-based International Transport Workers' Federation, commissioned an independent analysis. The federation's Mark Dickinson called the official commission's report "a political fix, concerned with appeasing vested interests, rather than identifying the circumstances surrounding the loss of the *Estonia* and establishing the causes by gathering information and drawing objective conclusions."[32] At the same time, numerous lawsuits were filed, with defendants and accusers citing findings from the various reports.

Send in the Go Team

In the United States, roughly five thousand accidents involving commercial vessels and eight thousand accidents involving recreational boats occur each year. The National Transportation Safety Board (NTSB) and the Coast Guard share responsibility for reviewing accidents that involve foreign vessels in U.S. territorial waters, or U.S. vessels anywhere in the world. Only major accidents involving deaths, serious damage to property or the environment, or accidents in which a great number of people were put at risk, as might be the case in a cruise ship accident, are formally investigated.

When a major accident involving U.S. ships occurs, the NTSB immediately dispatches a "Go Team" to the accident scene. Go Team members are experienced investigators from the NTSB's Washington, D.C., headquarters. They must be

◄ Coast Guard investigators check out a gaping hole in the hull of a ship after a 1999 collision.

ready to leave at a moment's notice for an accident scene that may be in nearby Chesapeake Bay or halfway around the world in the South China Sea. Depending on an investigator's area of expertise, the tools of their trade they pack along could include items as simple as flashlights and tape recorders, or as highly specialized as sonar equipment (which can provide information about undersea objects by bouncing sound waves off of them), high-resolution cameras, and diving gear.

The investigative team can number anywhere from three to more than a dozen people, depending on the seriousness of the accident. When investigators arrive on the scene, their

▶ Unmanned, remotely operated submersibles like this U.S. Navy Scorpio can play a vital role in investigations of sunken ships.

first task is to establish the facts about what happened. Witnesses are interviewed to reconstruct a detailed record of the accident and any evacuation and lifesaving procedures that took place. Testimony from eyewitnesses to an event is not completely reliable, however, and often conflicts with known facts or the testimony of other witnesses. According to a study by Great Britain's Marine Accident Investigation Bureau, human memory is so fallible that most people lose 50 percent of recall within half an hour. "Even the most cooperative of witnesses," says marine investigator John S. Lang, "will forget crucial events and will have difficulty in recalling precise times. Most witnesses do their best to remember events but there will be many gaps in the information they can provide."[33]

The investigative team, which can include marine engineers, naval architects, meteorologists, and survival specialists, also looks at the qualifications of crew members, the training they have received, their workload, and any factors that might lead to human error, such as fatigue, stress, long hours, medical conditions, or use of alcohol or drugs. Investigators collect documents pertaining to ship inspections and repair records. Engineers examining the wreckage of a collision may calculate impact angles and forces. Others gather information on the weather, listen to any ship-to-ship or ship-to-shore communications, and collect evidence from any computers or electronic devices onboard.

At the Bottom

An investigation is complicated when a ship has sunk in deep water, and even more so when all hands are lost. Dive teams are employed if the wreck is accessible, to recover bodies and to examine the boat to try to determine what happened. Specialized equipment, including manned submersibles, remote-controlled robotics, sonar devices, and high-definition video systems, may also be employed. Even so, the challenges faced are legion, including the tremendous depths some ships sink to, the extreme pressure and darkness at the bottom of the sea, and powerful undersea currents that can scatter evidence. All the equipment and expertise in the world does not necessarily guarantee that the cause of a disaster can be determined.

One of the most difficult investigations the NTSB has had to undertake involved the 729-foot *Edmund Fitzgerald*, which suddenly and mysteriously went to the bottom of Lake Superior on November 10, 1975. The ship, carrying twenty-six thousand tons of ore on a run from Superior, Wisconsin, to Detroit, Michigan, encountered a storm that gradually worsened. Battling ninety-mile-per-

BLACK BOXES OF THE SEA

A ship's voyage data recorder (VDR) is similar to the "black box" carried on commercial airplanes. The VDR automatically records conversations on the bridge as well as any communication between the ship and other stations. The device also keeps tabs on the ship's position, speed, compass and depth readings, alarm information, and radar data. Such information can enable accident investigators to review a ship crew's procedures and instructions before and during an incident, helping to identify the cause. VDRs are now required by the International Maritime Organization on passenger ships, on roll-on/roll-off ferries, and on cargo ships traveling internationally or within the European Union.

hour winds and thirty-foot-high waves, the *Fitzgerald*'s captain, Ernest McSorley, made radio contact with a nearby ship. He reported that the *Fitzgerald* had "a 'bad list,' had lost both radars, and was taking heavy seas over the deck in one of the worst seas he had ever been in." At 7:10 P.M. the *Fitzgerald* radioed to another ship, "We are holding our own."[34] Shortly afterwards, the *Edmund Fitzgerald* simply disappeared, without sending a single signal for help. All twenty-nine crew members went down with the ship.

The investigation into the sinking of the *Edmund Fitzgerald* took three years, and the final report covered seven volumes. Bad weather conditions and the fact that the wreckage

▼ A U.S. Navy admiral (left) and a ship's captain, members of the official inquiry into the sinking of the *Edmund Fitzgerald*, inspect debris from the ship.

was lying in 530 feet of water meant dive teams could not reach the wreckage until six months after the ship sank. An unmanned, deep-diving vehicle controlled from the surface and capable of television and still photography made twelve dives totaling more than fifty-six hours. The submersible recorded more than forty thousand feet of videotape and close to one thousand still color photographs. The investigating board concluded that water poured through leaking hatches. The ship developed a list and storm waves swamped it.

The finding was extremely controversial. Many people in the shipping community believed that the *Edmund Fitzgerald* had scraped bottom while navigating a more protected route it had taken to avoid the storm. The scraping may have caused flooding and eventual foundering. A diving expedition in 1995 found no evidence of a breach in the hull, but the cause of the sinking remains a mystery.

Investigating the *Arctic Rose*

In some instances the amount of information investigators can gather under such extremely difficult circumstances—no survivors, and a ship at the bottom of the sea—is astonishing. At 3:35 A.M. on April 2, 2001, the Coast Guard received an EPIRB emergency signal from the *Arctic Rose*. The ninety-two-foot fishing and fish-processing vessel was roughly two hundred miles offshore in the Bering Sea, too far for a helicopter search-and-rescue team to reach. Rescue planes arrived on the scene by about 7:00 A.M. but found nothing but a slight debris field.

"It was the worst fishing vessel casualty in fifty years due to the number of casualties; all fifteen crew members were lost," said Jim Robertson, a member of the Coast Guard investigative team based in Alaska. "The fact that the vessel sank with no survivors made the investigation particularly challenging."[35]

The first task was to find the wreckage. Sonar technicians scanning the bottom located the boat about four hundred feet down. A remote-operated vehicle was sent down several times to photograph and videotape the wreckage.

"We could see that there was no hull damage," Robertson says. "From the impact in the sand, we could tell that the vessel struck stern first and then landed upright." He adds:

They weren't fishing at the time, and the rudder was turned hard to port, which means they were probably listing to starboard. The aft weather tight door was open, which allowed water to flood into the processing space. The National Weather Service performed a "hindcast" using computer models, and concluded that the vessel foundered in twenty-five-foot seas or perhaps greater. Experts testifying at the hearing estimated that the open door allowed two to three tons of water per second to flood into the enclosed processing space. The effect of the water sloshing back and forth in rough seas would cause the boat to lose stability and sink quickly.[36]

Robertson notes that testimony suggested that fatigue may have been a factor in the sinking. The fish processors—most very young, a few on their first voyage—had been working fifteen-hour days for close to two months. "This could easily lead to a lack of attention to detail—like leaving a door open at night—which became a major causal factor in the sinking."[37]

Coast Guard investigators also compiled testimony and documentation of the history of the *Arctic Rose* itself, from her beginnings as a shrimping boat in the Gulf of Mexico through many subsequent identities. Ultimately, the investigation included testimony from former crew members, naval architects, engineers, boat inspectors, and boat owners to piece together the error chain. It overcame a number of difficulties to achieve its main goal: to make recommendations that can help prevent future accidents.

CHAPTER FIVE

Preventing Shipwrecks

W hen it comes to avoiding shipwrecks, humanity has progressed a long way from vaguely drawn maps, navigation by the stars, and the occasional lighthouse. Global mapping and location systems using satellites have taken much of the guesswork out of navigation, and high-tech equipment such as radar, depth gauges, and computers give ship captains more precise information about their surroundings. Television monitors can provide constant oversight of below-deck areas on a boat, and alarms alert a ship's crew to leaks or fires. Modern communication gear can notify authorities of a ship in distress in a matter of minutes. Considerable improvements in safety equipment have been made.

Such advances have reduced some of the common causes of collisions, fires, and groundings. For various reasons, however, shipwrecks have not been eliminated. Weather is a constant wild card. All the sophisticated new navigational and communication equipment must be installed and maintained, and crew members must be trained in its correct use. Because of cost considerations, many sectors of the shipping industry remain resistant to innovations and regulations that could further aid shipwreck prevention. Nevertheless preventive efforts have made important strides in reducing the sometimes tragic consequences of venturing out to sea.

Responding to Tragedies

As recently as 150 years ago, an ocean crossing was dangerous and time-consuming. Few standards governed ship construction and operation, no laws controlled crew training, and very little thought was given to safety equipment. Passengers knew they were taking their lives in their hands, and most traveled only when it was absolutely necessary. Gradually, as ship voyages became more popular, legislation designed to improve marine safety was put in place, but usually it took a major tragedy to spur lawmakers on.

Thus, the boiler explosion on the *Sultana* in April 1865, which took the lives of as many as eighteen hundred Union soldiers, led to legislation relating to ship construction techniques and materials. In response to the sinking of the *Titanic*, the first International Conference on Safety of Life at Sea (SOLAS) was convened in London in November 1913. The conference addressed such issues as the adequacy of existing lifeboat requirements, hull subdivision, and the necessity of twenty-four-hour radio communication coverage on passenger ships, and resulted in improved safety measures for international passenger ships.

Two accidents occurring relatively close together—the *Morro Castle* burning off the coast of New Jersey in September 1934, and a collision between the *Mohawk* and the *Talisman* that killed forty-five people in January 1935—spurred the U.S. Congress to pass the U.S. Merchant Marine Act of 1936, regulating the structure, equipment, and building materials for passenger ships. For example, fire-resisting bulkheads (barriers) on decks were required at certain intervals, a type of "passive" fire protection that was supposed to complement firefighting equipment. (Other countries, such as Britain, continued to emphasize "active" systems, such as automatic sprinklers.) The legislation also defined training requirements for officers and crew and required, for the first time, that marine casualties involving regulated vessels be reported and investigated to determine cause and to prevent recurrences.

A SMALL TRAGEDY BUT MAJOR CONSEQUENCES

Even small tragedies can lead to major safety-related overhauls. In 1997 a father, his two sons, and a nephew planned to sail from South Carolina to Florida on the thirty-four-foot sailboat *Morning Dew*. Around 2 A.M. of December 29 the boat crashed into a jetty on the north end of Charleston Harbor. One of the boys sent a frantic Mayday call, but it was ignored as "unintelligible" at the local Coast Guard station. Four hours later, when another ship reported hearing cries in the water to the Coast Guard, the agency again failed to respond. It was not until 11 A.M., when the bodies of two boys washed ashore, that the Coast Guard launched a search and rescue effort. It was too late to save either of the other two *Morning Dew* passengers. A subsequent investigation led to a multimillion-dollar revamping of Coast Guard's internal communication systems.

A Blow to Romance and Luxury

More than a decade later, one of the worst cruise ship fires in history prompted further safety reforms in a number of countries. The fire occurred on September 16, 1949, while the *Noronic*, the "Queen of the Inland Seas," was docked during a layover in Toronto. The largest and most luxurious Great Lakes passenger cruiser, it had perhaps six hundred passengers and their visitors onboard, plus only sixteen crew, at 2:30 A.M. when a fire started in a linen closet. Within ten minutes the upper decks were an inferno, with the ship's fine wood furnishings and partitions acting as fuel. Plus, as writer Chris Edwards notes, "The presence of long passageways and staircases that acted as chimneys increased [the ship's] vulnerability. All this practically guaranteed that once any fire started, it would sweep through the vessel with the explosive force of a blow torch."[38]

▲ A person injured in the collision between the liner *Mohawk* and the freighter *Talisman* is brought ashore from a Coast Guard rescue vessel in Staten Island, New York.

▲ The inferno onboard the *Noronic* while it was docked in Toronto was among the worst of the fires that have plagued the cruise industry.

As desperate passengers jumped seventy feet into the water, firefighters struggled to control the blaze, which burned so hot that water from fire hoses was being vaporized before it reached the hull. The final death toll was 118, with some bodies being almost completely cremated. Investigations pointed to management and shipboard complacency about the possibility of fire.

Media coverage of the spectacular blaze led to a major falloff in the Great Lakes cruise industry. "The era of associating romance and luxury with cruising on the Great Lakes came to a close with the S.S. *Noronic* disaster when the public instead began to associate fear with cruising,"[39] according to Tracy London of the Vancouver-based Oceans Blue Foundation.

Making Cruise Ships Safe

The fire on the *Noronic* had begun to fade in people's memories when two more disasters, the burning of the Greek cruise ship *Lakonia* on December 22, 1963, which killed 128 people, and the deadly 1965 *Yarmouth Castle* fire, again acted to hinder the development of the modern oceangoing cruise industry. These incidents led to further fire-prevention reforms that addressed issues such as combustible materials and the separation of accommodation spaces from machinery and cargo.

Gradually, the cruise industry recovered, and since the 1980s it has skyrocketed. The Coast Guard estimates that 130 or so major cruise ships (nearly all of which are registered under flags of various foreign countries) operating from U.S. ports carried more than 7 million passengers in 2001. A cruise industry trade association has forecast growth worldwide to 20 million passengers annually by 2010. The ships are being built on an ever-larger scale—Royal Caribbean Cruise Line's flagship (the largest in its fleet) *Voyager of the Seas* can accommodate more than five thousand passengers and crew.

Within recent years these expensive, high-tech vessels have generally averted major disasters, in part because they avoid extreme weather—vacationers prefer the sun—and they are fast enough to outrun the approach of a hurricane. On the other hand, like their precursors, the great liners, they have proven to be stubbornly vulnerable to fire. A relatively few such incidents have claimed large numbers of lives since the 1980s. In particular, a deadly cruise ship fire occurred on April 7, 1990, while the *Scandinavian Star* was en route from Oslo, Norway, to Frederikshavn, Denmark. Within forty-five minutes, 158 people died, most of smoke inhalation. Many victims were found in their cabins on lower decks, where they apparently did not hear alarm bells or were not awakened by the crew. The investigation by several Scandinavian nations found that the crew was unprepared and untrained to deal with a fire emergency, and that fire and safety equipment was missing, inoperable, or poorly maintained. The fire prompted the International Marine Organization to draft additional fire safety requirements.

The question of smoke detectors in cabins is a fire-prevention issue that illustrates the problem of

 FLAGS OF INCONVENIENCE

Implementing and enforcing safety measures in the United States has been hampered by the fact that many ships operate under "flags of convenience." By registering a ship in countries such as Panama, Liberia, and the Bahamas, ship owners can avoid the stricter inspection requirements and safety regulations, as well as the higher taxes and registration fees, found in countries such as the United States and Great Britain. Many of the ships sailing under flags of convenience adhere to only the minimum safety and hiring practices required under international law. They also hire employees with little or no training, pay them poorly, and sometimes even abandon sailors in distant ports when aging ships get too expensive to run.

regulating an international industry. U.S. laws require that all passenger cabins be fitted with smoke alarms similar to those found in hotel rooms. U.S. law, however, applies only to vessels registered in the United States. Most cruise ships operate in international waters and are registered outside the United States. After a series of fire incidents aboard cruise ships, including the July 1996 Panamanian-flag *Universe Explorer* fire off Alaska, in which five crewmen died of smoke inhalation and sixty-seven crew members and two passengers were injured, the NTSB recommended that foreign flag cruise ships install such alarms. The alarms are not required under international law, however, and the cruise ship industry has resisted implementing the recommendations. Cruise lines argue that having alarms sound in passenger accommodation areas could lead to panic over false alarms. Cost is also an issue.

Abandon Ship

With more than 7 million people leaving U.S. ports on cruises each year, passenger evacuation procedures have received a great deal of attention recently. The danger from fire is exacerbated when evacuation procedures are faulty or not clearly spelled out. Many of the deaths that occurred on the *Scandinavian Star* were attributed to unclear signs directing passengers to exits. The IMO cites evacuation as a major concern in cruise ships today. Ships carrying several thousand people face inherent logistical problems, and these problems are compounded by the fact that cruises often include many older people, some of whom may be disabled.

Innumerable ship evacuations have been compromised when crew members do not speak the same language as passengers, as is frequently the case on cruise ships flying under flags of convenience. U.S. law requires that crew members at critical stations speak English, but in the event of an emergency, passengers are more likely to encounter hotel-type employees like room stewards rather than sailors responsible for manning key positions. Even when passengers have been successfully evacuated from a ship, problems remain for search-and-rescue teams faced with transferring hundreds or even thousands of people unfamiliar with ships and the sea, from crowded lifeboats to vessels that can transport them to land.

Rescuers dealt successfully with this challenge when, in the early morning hours of October 4, 1980, a fire erupted in

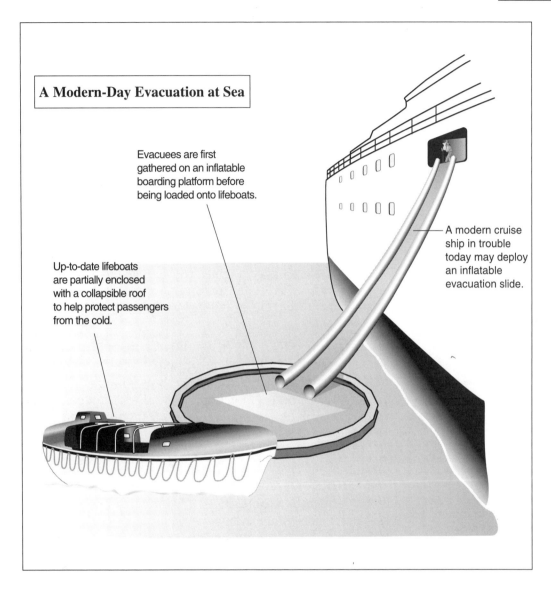

A Modern-Day Evacuation at Sea

Evacuees are first gathered on an inflatable boarding platform before being loaded onto lifeboats.

A modern cruise ship in trouble today may deploy an inflatable evacuation slide.

Up-to-date lifeboats are partially enclosed with a collapsible roof to help protect passengers from the cold.

the engine room of the Dutch cruise ship *Prinsendam* as it was sailing 120 miles off the coast of Alaska. The fire spread rapidly out of control, and at 6:30 A.M. the order to abandon ship was given. Passengers and crew were all safely evacuated into lifeboats, but in the rough seas and heavy weather, many passengers suffered from hypothermia and exposure. During the subsequent investigation, passengers complained that they were not given adequate notice of the nature and extent of the emergency. As a result many abandoned ship in light clothing, and were not prepared for the weather conditions they encountered in the open lifeboats. Passengers also complained that some of the crew left the vessel before they did and were first into the rescue helicopters that hoisted people from the lifeboats. The fact that no one died attests to the efforts of the rescue forces on the scene.

Rescue procedures and technologies have advanced significantly since the familiar open rowboats of the *Titanic*. Some ships now have evacuation chutes, similar to those used to remove passengers from airliners during an emergency. In a review of international safety reforms relating to lifesaving systems, the Coast Guard comments:

> Today's lifeboats have full or partial rigid enclosures to protect the occupants from the elements, and are propelled by diesel engines. Lifeboats on tankers are equipped with air supply and sprinkler systems which allow them to travel through fire on the water. Many cargo ships have a free-fall launched lifeboat that is dropped from a ramp on the stern of the ship.[40]

In 2000 the IMO initiated a multiyear study of safety procedures on cruise ships, and the principles of successful evacuations on land are being applied to ships. Among the factors that affect evacuation in general are the width of corridors, crowd size and density, and emergency planning and training. Additional factors that impact a successful ship evacuation include the speed at which the ship sinks, weather conditions, onboard communications to passengers, and the timely arrival of rescuers. A study by Indiana University psychology professor Jerome Chertkoff compared twelve famous cases of unsuccessful passenger evacuations, like those of the *Titanic* and the *Lusitania*, and four successful evacuations, including those of the *Republic* in 1909 and the *Andrea Doria* in 1956. His analysis has identified more than a dozen factors that can make the difference between life and death in the evacuation of passenger ships. The results of his study will be useful to ship architects and safety professionals.

Improving the Floating Coffins

Ferries have proven to be arguably much more dangerous than cruise ships, and preventing ferry disasters is one of the most difficult problems facing maritime officials. Substandard ships, badly trained crews, and a lack of industry regulation in many developing countries contribute to frequent catastrophes. Many ferries operate in the waters of a single country, and thus are not subject to international laws. National laws can range from nonexistent to inadequate, or the laws exist but are simply not enforced. In the Philippines, for example, where ferries are often rickety and under-serviced, government inspections are performed infrequently. As a result, the country suffers roughly one hundred ferry accidents a year. Many of these involve high numbers of fatalities, though thankfully there has not been a repeat of the 1987 *Dona Paz* sinking with fatalities numbering in the thousands.

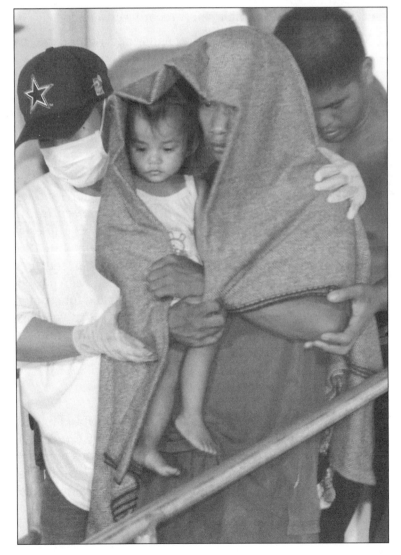

◄ Survivors of a May 2003 ferry sinking in the Philippines that killed at least twenty-five people are escorted off of a rescue vessel.

Addressing the problem of overcrowding would reduce the scope of ferry disasters, but progress is slow. Philippine guidelines allow ships to exceed their usual capacity by 10 percent during rush times. In practice, the 10 percent figure is often stretched further—the *Dona Paz*'s manifest listed 1,493 passengers and 50 crew members, yet more than 4,000 are thought to have perished. In addition to being hideously overcrowded, passenger baggage, which includes everything from hand-carried items to farm animals, often clutters passageways and blocks corridors. This can present deadly obstacles during an emergency. Enforcing limits on passengers' loads could help the Philippines emulate Hong Kong, notes writer Marc Lerner, where ferries carry more than 150,000 people every day with an admirable safety record. Lerner adds:

> Vessels there are subjected to regular and rigorous inspections, and operators face heavy fines and the revocation of their licenses for safety violations. Also, officials there generally can't be bribed. "What's needed in the Philippines is the political will to enforce the rules and see that punishments are meted out to those who break them," said one maritime expert. "That hasn't been the case in the past."[41]

National and international guidelines developed in the 1990s also addressed the issue of unsafe ro-ro ferries. The 1987 sinking of the British ferry *Herald of Free Enterprise* off the coast of Belgium prompted Great Britain, for example, to introduce a requirement that ferries have cameras fitted to the front of ships so that captains on the bridge can see on a monitor whether the loading doors have indeed been closed before sailing. International rules have also called for stricter construction standards, better onboard securing of vehicles and cargo to prevent dangerous shifting, and more training for officers and crew members.

Rebuilding Oil Tankers

The first oil spill prevention convention was adopted by the IMO in 1954, but it was the wreck of the *Torrey Canyon* in 1967 that pointed to the need for sweeping changes to international standards. When the *Exxon Valdez* ran aground in 1989, leaking 11 million gallons of oil into Alaska's Prince William Sound, the U.S. Congress responded by passing the

SEEING BELOW THE SURFACE

Accurately determining the depth of water beneath a ship's hull is a major factor in preventing groundings. Until almost the twentieth century, the main method used was quite simple, if not particularly accurate: Sailors tied lead weights to a rope segmented by knots and threw it overboard. Charts showing sea depths, known as bathymetric maps, gradually became available; some of the earliest were published in 1584. Currents and wave action mean that sandbars and shoals are constantly changing, however, making maps useful as a guide at best.

During the early twentieth century incidents like the grounding of the *Princess May* remained all too common. The passenger and cargo ship was running at close to full speed at high tide during a heavy fog when she ran into the rocky outcroppings of Sentinel Island, Alaska, early in the morning of August 5, 1910. Everyone onboard was safely evacuated, but the ship remained beached for nearly a month before tugboats could drag her off the rocks and refloat her.

It would not be until the 1920s, when sonar depth sounders became common equipment on vessels of various sizes, that captains had an effective technology to help prevent groundings.

▲ Modern depth-defining technologies can help avert groundings like that of the *Princess May* in 1910.

▲ Volunteers help to clean up oil that washed ashore in northern Spain after the tanker *Prestige* broke up.

Oil Pollution Act of 1990. The act ushered in a new safety regime for seaborne oil transport, and mandated the phasing out of conventional, single-hull tankers. It also required that the oil industry take greater precautions against spills and prepare detailed emergency response plans for cleaning up spills that occur.

The IMO followed with similar regulations two years later. By 2010, all tankers and supertankers carrying crude oil must have double hulls—a second, inner layer of steel separated by empty space from the outer hull. Currently, however, thousands of single-hull oil and chemical tankers still ply the seas.

Pressure is mounting for tougher inspections of tankers and for restrictions on their movement to protect vulnerable ecosystems. In 1997 nearly 49 million gallons of oil spilled into the world's waters and onto its shores in 136 incidents, according to the *Oil Spill Intelligence Report*, a research publication that keeps track of spills. Coordinating and enforcing an international effort to cut back on the number of oil spills remains difficult, however, because shipping regulations, environmental awareness, and safety procedures vary widely from country to country. In addition, attempts to put stronger certification and inspection procedures in place are regularly thwarted by the influence of Liberia and other flag-of-convenience nations. They have considerable influence within the IMO because they contribute much of the agency's funding, which is tied to a formula based on ship tonnage among the registered member states. It has been possible for just six flag-of-convenience states to stop IMO rules from being adopted.

When Ports Pull Up the Welcome Mat

Lacking the ability to control shipboard safety, a number of countries have begun to mandate such policies by controlling ships' access to ports. Refusal of docking privileges can have a devastating economic effect on operators of cruise ships as well as container ships. Some ports of call are banning certain ships—or shipping lines—that have extremely bad reputations. These efforts have had some beneficial effects. Ships with reputations for dumping refuse, or for having inadequate equipment to move oil from ship to shore, have been refused docking privileges, forcing them to halt such practices or upgrade their equipment. The Port of Seattle has been particularly successful in cleaning up its waters.

The practice can backfire though, as seen in the November 2002 saga of the *Prestige*. The 979-foot, twenty-six-year-old tanker developed a crack in its single hull when it was caught in high winds and tall waves thirty miles off the coast of Spain. With his ship listing and beginning to lose oil, the Greek captain of the vessel asked Spanish and Portuguese authorities for a port of refuge so that he could off-load his cargo and make repairs. Permission was denied and he was told to leave Spanish waters. While the *Prestige* was being hauled out to sea by tugboats, the crack widened. The ship broke in two and sank, spilling 20 million gallons of heavy fuel oil.

Oil eventually reached the coastlines of Spain, Portugal, and France. Tens of thousands of birds, marine animals, and other wildlife died, and fisheries collapsed. Cleanup costs for the accident are expected to run to hundreds of millions of dollars. Much of the bill will have to be picked up by the citizens of Spain, Portugal, and France, since insurance carried

CLEANING UP AN OIL SPILL

Once oil has spilled, cleanup often falls to local and federal government agencies, industry, and to volunteer organizations. The first tool used to mop up spilled oil is often a boom, a floating barrier to contain the oil. Then sponges, skimmers, and vacuums may be used to pull the spilled oil from the water surface. In some instances chemical dispersants can promote dilution of oil in water, and biological agents can break down the oil into its chemical constituents. Washing oil off of beaches is a dirty and time-consuming chore, even with the help of high-pressure water hoses. Cleanup workers on the shore may also turn to shovels and road equipment to move oil-laden sand and gravel to where it can be cleaned by being tumbled around in the waves.

by the *Prestige* amounted to only $25 million. (The International Oil Pollution Compensation Fund, funded by oil-consuming nations, may contribute an extra $180 million.)

In response to the entire disaster, in December 2002 European Union (EU) transport ministers agreed to ban single-hull oil tankers from EU ports, starting in 2010. In the interim, such vessels older than twenty-three years of age carrying heavy crude oil, and certain other highly polluting forms of oil, were immediately banned from calling at EU ports. The EU also released a "blacklist" of sixty-six ships that have been detained on several occasions in European ports for failing to comply with maritime safety rules. The hope is that operators will refrain from chartering substandard ships and that the owners and flag states of the ships in question will be forced to adopt the tougher maritime safety standards.

Recent laws that place liability for oil spills squarely on the oil companies have fueled the commercial development of a variety of innovations to stem the flow of oil once a ship's hull has been breached. These include a neoprene "Magnapatch," a sort of bandage for crippled ships, and techniques that use hydrostatic pressure to contain oil in a breached hull.

Protecting Commercial Fishermen

The commercial fishing industry is the most dangerous place to work in the United States. Every year close to one hundred fishermen die at sea, and commercial fishing boats have a fatality rate that is more than five times higher than other domestic commercial vessels.

Narrow profit margins are a major contributing factor to the level of danger. "A [fisherman] has three major enemies at sea: storms, mechanical failure, and his own hunger for success,"[42] writes Douglas A. Campbell in *The Sea's Bitter Harvest*, a book chronicling a thirteen-day period in January 1999, when four commercial clam boats sank with ten lives lost. Many of the waters in the United States have been overfished, and fishing seasons have been shortened to conserve species. The shortened seasons force fishermen to go out in weather they might previously have avoided. To keep costs down, fishermen frequently gloss over routine maintenance while on shore, and overload their boats, destabilizing them, while at sea.

Coast Guard and NTSB safety experts have long said that commercial fishermen in general lack an appreciation of principles of ship stability. Captains and crews frequently operate by "gut" as much as anything else, and while overloading under ordinary conditions does not pose a problem, an overloaded boat in a major storm can prove catastrophic. Accident reports often cite the need for regulations that would require fishing vessels to be weighed and inspected after modifications have been made. The commercial fishing industry,

▼ Handling heavy and unwieldy traps is typical of the hazardous tasks that make commercial crab fishing so dangerous.

RETURN
FUEL LIN

▲ In November 2000 a marine safety expert investigates the cause of an engine room fire aboard a ninety-two-foot, Alaska-based fishing vessel.

however, has historically opposed government regulation because of the added costs imposed by safety requirements. As a result, the United States has no mandatory requirements for inspections of fishing boats or equipment, and no licensing or certification requirements for captains or crews of fishing vessels.

The leading contributing factors to fishing vessel casualties are inadequate preparation for emergencies, poor vessel and/or safety equipment conditions, and lack of awareness of, or ignoring, stability issues. The Coast Guard has recommended boat safety inspections, but at the moment compliance is voluntary and fewer than 15 percent of the commercial fishing fleet participates. A similar lack of regulatory effectiveness exists at the international level, which means that disasters involving commercial fishing vessels are likely to remain all too common in the near future.

An Uncertain Future

For much of human history sailors embarked on sea journeys relying on little more than blind courage, boundless faith, and hard-earned experience. Today, computers, radar, satellites, and other advances in technology and ship design supplement bravery and wisdom. But accidents can never be completely eliminated. Phasing out older and substandard ships—especially aging oil tankers and passenger ferries—will help. But the human factor is crucial in reducing collisions, groundings, onboard fires, and other maritime accidents. And humans will continue to make mistakes, ignoring critical information, taking calculated risks that go wrong, daring the sea to seize and destroy—which, unfortunately, the sea will at times continue to do.

Notes

Introduction: Peril at Sea

1. Quoted in Edward S. Kamuda, "Titanic: Past and Present," *Titanic Historical Society*. www.titanic1.org.
2. Quoted in Charles Pellegrino, *Ghosts of the Titanic*. New York: HarperCollins, 2000, p. 97.
3. Charles Perrow, *Normal Accidents: Living with High-Risk Technologies*. Princeton, NJ: Princeton University Press, 1999, pp. 173–174.

Chapter 1: The Ship Goes Down

4. Quoted in "Program Description," Rescue at Sea, *PBS Online*. www.pbs.org.
5. Quoted in Don Lynch, *Titanic: An Illustrated History*. Toronto: Madison Press Books, 1992, p. 80.
6. Quoted in Daniel Allen Butler, *"Unsinkable": The Full Story of RMS Titanic*. Mechanicsburg, PA: Stackpole Books, 1998, p. 66.
7. James R. Chiles, *Inviting Disaster: Lessons from the Edge of Technology*. New York: HarperBusiness, 2001, p. 85.
8. Quoted in Butler, *"Unsinkable,"* p. 94.
9. H.D.S. Greenway, "Is It Safe?" *Boston Globe Magazine*, July 27, 2003, p. 24.
10. Quoted in "Submission of TUAC to the UNEP Industry Sector Reports: Transport," Division of Technology, Industry, and Economics, *United Nations Environment Programme*. www.uneptie.org.

Chapter 2: Surviving a Catastrophe

11. Quoted in Russell Smith, "The Sinking of the *Andrea Doria*," *Sweetwater Reporter News*, July 25, 1990. www.kerbow.com.
12. William Hoffer, *Saved! The Story of the Andrea Doria*. New York: Summit Books, 1979, p. 87.

13. Quoted in Nick Messinger, "The Canadian Pacific's SS *Princess Sophia*," *Nick Messinger's Homepage.* www.nickmessinger.co.uk.

14. "The Experiences of a Hawthorne Nurse, As Told by Miss Repa, Hawthorne Hospital," *Eastland Memorial Society.* www.eastlandmemorial.org.

Chapter 3: How Accidents Happen

15. Chiles, *Inviting Disaster*, p. 3.

16. Quoted in "The Medusa," *TLC.com.* http://tlc.discovery.com.

17. Butler, *"Unsinkable"*, p. 250.

18. Perrow, *Normal Accidents*, p. 177.

19. Quoted in "Empress of Ireland," Lost Liners, *PBS Online.* www.pbs.org.

20. Quoted in Douglas Campbell, *The Sea's Bitter Harvest.* New York: Carrol & Graf, 2002, p. 196.

21. Quoted in William Kornblum, "The *General Slocum* Disaster," The Hell Gate, *NewYorkHistory.info.* www.newyorkhistory.info.

22. K.M. Varghese, "Marine Accident Investigators International Forum," *Taiwan Institute of Transportation.* www.iot.gov.tw.

Chapter 4: Investigations at Sea

23. John S. Lang, "Report to United Kingdom Marine Accident Investigation Branch," Marine Accident Investigation Branch, *Department for Transport.* www.dft.gov.uk.

24. Quoted in Diana Preston, *Lusitania: An Epic Tragedy.* New York: Walker, 2002, p. 91.

25. Quoted in Preston, *Lusitania*, p. 195.

26. Preston, *Lusitania*, p. 308.

27. Quoted in Preston, *Lusitania*, p. 307.

28. Quoted in Preston, *Lusitania*, pp. 307–308.

29. Quoted in Preston, *Lusitania*, p. 294.

30. Quoted in Colin Boyd, "*Herald of Free Enterprise* Car Ferry Disaster," University of South Australia Division of Business and Enterprise. http://business.unisa.edu.au.

31. Quoted in "Report: Design Flaw Led to *Estonia* Ferry Sinking," *CNN.com*, December 3, 1997. www.cnn.com.

32. Quoted in "ITF Demands New 'Estonia' Investigation," *International Transport Workers' Federation*. www.itf. org.uk.

33. Lang, "Report to United Kingdom Marine Accident Investigation Branch."

34. Quoted in National Transportation Safety Board, "Marine Accident Report: SS *Edmund Fitzgerald* Sinking in Lake Superior, November 10, 1975," No. NTSB-MAR-78-3, *U.S. Coast Guard*. www.uscg.mil.

35. Jim Robertson, interview by the author, July 25, 2003.

36. Robertson, interview.

37. Robertson, interview.

Chapter 5: Preventing Shipwrecks

38. Chris Edwards, "The Burning of the *Noronic*," *Walkerville Times*. www.walkervilletimes.com.

39. Tracy London, "'Blowing the Whistle' and the Case for Cruise Certification," *Oceans Blue Foundation*. www.oceansblue.org.

40. *U.S. Coast Guard*, "What Is 'SOLAS'?" www.uscg.mil.

41. Marc Lerner, "Philippine Ferry Collision Hardens Safety Calls," *Washington Times*, May 30, 2003. www. washtimes.com.

42. Campbell, *The Sea's Bitter Harvest*, p. 60.

Glossary

aft: Toward the back of a ship.

bathymetric map: A chart showing water depth at various places.

boiler: A large, typically wood- or coal-burning furnace that heats water to create steam to power ships.

bow: The front end of a ship.

bridge: The raised platform near the front of a ship from which it is navigated.

crow's nest: The lookout platform at or near the top of a mast.

davits: The cranelike arms used for holding and lowering lifeboats.

EPIRB: Emergency Position Indicating Radio Beacon, which sends a signal alerting the Coast Guard that the vessel is in trouble.

forward: Toward the front of a ship.

hypothermia: A loss of body heat that can happen quickly in water and become life threatening.

knot: A unit of speed equivalent to one nautical mile per hour or 1.15 miles per hour.

list: When a ship is leaning to one side or the other.

port: The left side of a ship when facing forward.

purser: An offical on a ship responsible for papers and accounts.

rogue wave: A wave that can appear out of nowhere and tower up to ninety feet high.

ro-ro: Short for "roll-on/roll-off," referring to a ferry that typically opens in the bow and stern to load and unload vehicles, cargo, and passengers.

sandbar: A ridge of sand formed in a river or along a shore by the action of waves or currents.

shoal: A shallow place or a sandy elevation in a body of water that makes navigation hazardous.

sonar: A method or device for using reflected sound waves to locate objects underwater.

starboard: The right side of a ship when facing foward.

steamboat: A vessel powered by steam generated in boilers.

stern: The rear end of a ship.

wave height: The vertical distance between the crest and trough of a wave.

wireless: A communication technology using radio signals to transmit information.

For Further Reading

Books

Caroline Alexander, *The Endurance: Shackleton's Legendary Antarctic Expedition.* New York: Alfred A. Knopf, 1998. Story of the explorer's expedition to Antarctica, being stranded, and the miraculous rescue, with stunning photographs.

Robert B. Ballard, *GhostLiners.* Boston: Little, Brown, 1998. Provides brief histories of the sinking of the *Titanic, Lusitania, Empress of Ireland*, and others.

Daniel Allen Butler, *"Unsinkable": The Full Story of RMS Titanic.* Mechanicsburg, PA: Stackpole Books, 1998. A well-researched and thoroughly readable narrative.

Don Lynch, *Titanic: An Illustrated History.* Toronto: Madison Press Books, 1992. The story of the *Titanic* told in photos as well as dramatic paintings by Ken Marschall.

David Ritchie, *Shipwrecks: An Encyclopedia of the World's Worst Disasters at Sea.* New York: Checkmark Books, 1999. A fact-filled reference work.

Periodicals

Thomas B. Allen, "Remember the *Maine*?" *National Geographic*, February 1998.

Thomas L. Farnquist, "Requiem for the *Edmund Fitzgerald*," *National Geographic*, January 1996.

Internet Sources

Edward S. Kamuda, "*Titanic:* Past and Present," *Titanic Historical Society.* www.titanic1.org.

Websites

National Transportation Safety Board (www.ntsb.gov). Offers marine accident reports and numerous other resources.

United States Coast Guard (www.uscg.mil). The agency's official site.

Works Consulted

Books

Hal Burton, *The Morro Castle: Tragedy at Sea*. New York: Viking Press, 1973. A comprehensive history of the 1934 incident.

Douglas Campbell, *The Sea's Bitter Harvest*. New York: Carrol & Graf, 2002. The compelling story of four commercial fishing boats that sank in the Atlantic within thirteen days of one another in January 1999.

James R. Chiles, *Inviting Disaster: Lessons from the Edge of Technology*. New York: HarperBusiness, 2001. A look at disasters resulting from technological glitches compounded by human error.

William Hoffer, *Saved! The Story of the Andrea Doria*. New York: Summit Books, 1979. A comprehensive retelling of the sinking and rescue.

Alexander McKee, *Wreck of the Medusa: The Tragic Story of the Death Raft*. New York: Signet, 2000. Details the gruesome nineteenth-century disaster.

Charles Pellegrino, *Ghosts of the Titanic*. New York: Harper-Collins, 2000. A well-researched and up-to-date account.

Charles Perrow, *Normal Accidents: Living with High-Risk Technologies*. Princeton, NJ: Princeton University Press, 1999. Offers an excellent discussion of marine accidents.

Diana Preston, *Lusitania: An Epic Tragedy*. New York: Walker, 2002. Includes extensive coverage of the political ramifications, early submarine warfare, and role in World War I.

Periodicals

Robert D. Ballard, "High-Tech Search for Roman Shipwrecks," *National Geographic*, April 1998.

———, "How We Found *Titanic*," *National Geographic*, December 1985.

———,"Riddle of the *Lusitania*," *National Geographic*, April 1994.

H.D.S. Greenway, "Is It Safe?" *Boston Globe Magazine*, July 27, 2003.

Gary Stoller, "Despite Law, Fishermen Face Deadliest Job Risks," *USA Today*, March 12, 2003.

Internet Sources

Colin Boyd, "*Herald of Free Enterprise* Car Ferry Disaster," University of South Australia Division of Business and Enterprise. http://business.unisa.edu.au.

CNN.com, "Report: Design Flaw Led to *Estonia* Ferry Sinking," December 3, 1997. www.cnn.com.

Eastland Memorial Society, "The Experiences of a Hawthorne Nurse, As Told by Miss Repa, Hawthorne Hospital." www.eastlandmemorial.org.

Chris Edwards, "The Burning of the *Noronic*," *Walkerville Times*. www.walkervilletimes.com.

International Transport Workers' Federation, "ITF Demands New 'Estonia' Investigation." www.itf.org.uk.

William Kornblum, "The General Slocum Disaster," The Hell Gate, *NewYorkHistory.info*. www.newyorkhistory.info.

John S. Lang, "Report to United Kingdom Marine Accident Investigation Branch," Marine Accident Investigation Branch, *Department for Transport*. www.dft.gov.uk.

Marc Lerner, "Philippine Ferry Collision Hardens Safety Calls," *Washington Times*, May 30, 2003. www.washtimes.com.

Tracy London, "'Blowing the Whistle' and the Case for Cruise Certification," *Oceans Blue Foundation*. www.oceansblue.org.

Nick Messinger, "The Canadian Pacific's SS *Princess Sophia*," *Nick Messinger's Homepage*. www.nickmessinger.co.uk.

National Transportation Safety Board, "Marine Accident Report: Fire on Board the Liberian Passenger Ship *Ecstasy*, Miami, Florida, July 20, 1998," No. MAR-01/01. www.ntsb.gov.

———, "Marine Accident Report: Sinking of the Recreational Sailing Vessel *Morning Dew* at the Entrance to the Harbor of Charleston, South Carolina, December 29, 1997," No. MAR-99/01. www.ntsb.gov.

PBS Online, Lost Liners, "Empress of Ireland." www.pbs.org.

———, Rescue at Sea, "Program Description." www.pbs.org.

R.M.S. Titanic History, "The City of Boston." www. rmstitanichistory.com.

Russell Smith, "The Sinking of the Andrea Doria," *Sweetwater Reporter News*, July 25, 1990. www.kerbow.com.

TLC.com, "The Medusa." http://tlc.discovery.com.

United Nations Environment Programme, Division of Technology, Industry, and Economics, "Submission of TUAC to the UNEP Industry Sector Reports: Transport." www.uneptie.org.

University of Alaska Anchorage Information Technology Services, Alaska Oil Spill Commission, "Case Study of the Exxon Valdez Oil Spill." http://hosting.uaa. alaska.edu.

U.S. Coast Guard, "Marine Accident Report: SS *Edmund Fitzgerald* Sinking in Lake Superior, November 10, 1975," National Transportation Safety Board, No. NTSB-MAR-78-3. www.uscg.mil.

———, "What Is 'SOLAS'?" www.uscg.mil.

K.M. Varghese, "Marine Accident Investigators International Forum," *Taiwan Institute of Transportation*. www.iot.gov.tw.

Websites

Encyclopedia Titanica (www.encyclopedia-titanica.org). Extensive source of articles and background.

International Registry of Sunken Ships (http://users. accesscomm.ca/shipwreck). Worldwide shipwreck database.

TheShipsList (www.theshipslist.com). Offers ship descriptions, schedules, wreck data, voyage accounts, and other information.

Index

Aegean Captain (oil tanker), 27

Alaska Oil Spill Commission, 50

Albacore (submarine), 21

Allen, Thomas B., 66

Amoco Cadiz (oil tanker), 27

Andrea Doria (ocean liner), 28–34, 86
    situation for survivors onboard, 32–34

Andrea Gail (fishing vessel), 58

Arctic Rose (fishing vessel), 77–78

Atlantic Empress (oil tanker), 27

Ballard, Robert, 68–69

Balsa 37 (freighter), 53–54

Baltic, 38

bathymetric maps, 89

Battle of Ôland, 56

Binns, Jack, 38

Bismarck (battleship), 22

boilers, 56, 80

Bukoba (ferry), 20

Butler, Daniel Allen, 49–50

Calamai, Piero, 28–29, 32

Californian, 17

Campbell, Douglas A., 92–93

Captain Fred Bouchard (tug/barge), 53–54

Carlisle, Alexander, 18

Carnival Cruise Lines, 61

"Case Study of the *Exxon Valdez* Oil Spill," 50

Chertkoff, Jerome, 86

Chiles, James R., 17, 46

Civil War, 55–56

coastlines, dangerous, 13–14

collisions, 51–52. *see also Andrea Doria* (ocean liner)

in crowded ports, 53–54

between surface ships and submarines, 54

commercial fishing industry, 92–94
    opposition to government regulations by, 93–94

CQD (emergency code), 16

cruise ships
    blow to, 81–82
    fires onboard, 59, 80, 81–82, 83, 84, 85–86
    operating from U.S. ports, 83
    passenger evacuation procedures for, 84
    safety increased on, 82–84

Cunard Line, 67, 69

De Chaumereys, Hugues Duroy, 47–48

Dickinson, Mark, 72

Dickson, Kathy, 29

Dona Paz (ferry), 20–21, 34, 87–88

Eastland, 36–38

Ecstasy (cruise ship), 61

Edmund Fitzgerald (cargo ship), 75–77

Edwards, Chris, 81

Ehime Maru (fishing vessel), 54

Emergency Position Indicating Radio Beacons (EPIRBs), 39, 45, 77

Empress of Ireland (passenger ship), 51–52, 71

Endurance (wooden sailing ship), 34, 36

environment. *see also* oil spills
    need for increased international awareness of, 90–91
    threats posed by offshore disasters to, 25–27

Estonia (ferry), 56–57, 72

European Union (EU), 75
    "blacklist" of, 92

Exxon Valdez (oil tanker), 26, 50, 88

Fame (sailing ship), 58

ferries, 58, 60
    improving, 86–88
    as overcrowded floating coffins, 19–21
    phasing out older and substandard, 95
    problems associated with, 87–88
    ro-ro, 19, 56–57, 69–70, 72, 75

Finnpulp (freighter), 41

flags of convenience
    nations, influence on IMO of, 91

problems during emergencies caused by, 84
   relation of safety to, 83
Fleet, Frederick, 8
Florida (immigrant ship), 38

General Grant (sailing ship), 14
General Slocum (paddlewheel-powered excursion ferry), 58, 60
General Steuben (converted passenger ship), 23
Gericault, Theodore, 48
Goya, 23
Greenville (nuclear-powered submarine), 54
Greenway, H.D.S., 25
groundings, preventing, 89

Hart, Eva, 9–10
Herald of Free Enterprise (ferry), 69–70
   new requirements after sinking of, 88
Hoffer, William, 32
Hood (battle cruiser), 22
Horgan, John J., 67
hull, 82
   containing oil in breached, 92
   double, 90
   single, 90, 91–92
   subdivision, 80
hypothermia, 45, 52, 65, 85
   chart, 44

Ile de France (ocean liner), 33, 34
Imo (supply ship), 23–24
International Conference on Safety of Life at Sea (SOLAS), 80
International Maritime Organization (IMO), 70–71, 75
   drafting of additional fire safety requirements by, 83
   evacuation concerns of, 84
   influence of flag-of-convenience nations on, 91
   safety study initiated by, 86
International Oil Pollution Compensation Fund, 92
International Transport Workers' Federation, 72
investigations, 63–78
   Arctic Rose, 77–78
   Ecstasy, 61
   Edmund Fitzgerald, 75–77

Empress of Ireland, 71
Estonia, 72
Herald of Free Enterprise, 69–70
investigative teams, 72–75
jurisdictional issues, 70–72
Lusitania, 65, 67–69
Maine, 66
Morro Castle, 59
primary goal of modern shipwreck, 63
Storstad, 71
testimony of witnesses, 74
Inviting Disaster: Lessons from the Edge of Technology (Chiles), 17

Junger, Sebastian, 58

Kronan (warship), 56

L-3 (submarine), 23
Lakonia (cruise ship), 82
Lancastria (ocean liner), 21
Lang, John S., 63, 74
Lerner, Marc, 88
lifeboats, 8, 14, 51, 52, 59
   Andrea Doria, 29, 33–34
   inability to launch, 19
   problem of weather on open, 85–86
   requirements for, on passenger ships, 11
   Titanic, 9–10, 18
   today, 86
list, 9, 33, 36–37, 51, 76, 77, 77–78
Lloyd's (London insurance company), 12
London, Tracy, 82
Louis XVIII (king of France), 47
Lusitania: An Epic Tragedy (Preston), 65
Lusitania (ocean liner), 64–65, 67–69, 86
   first inquiry into, 65, 67
   Germany's torpedoing of, 65, 67
   new findings cloud tragedy of, 68–69

Maine (battleship), 66
Marine Accident Investigation Bureau (Great Britain), 74
marine disasters
   danger on land from, 23–25
   increased potential for harbor accidents due to, 24–25

resulting from acts of war, 21–23, 64–65, 67–69
threat to environment from, 25–27. *see also* oil spills
Marine Electric, 43
Marques (sail-training ship), 15
Mason, J. Cass, 56
Massachusetts Humane Society, 39
Maxtone-Graham, John, 16
Mayday, 16
call, unheeded, 80
Mayo Clinic, 44
McKee, Alexander, 47
McKinley, William, 66
McSorley, Ernest, 76
Medusa, 47–48
Mersey, Lord, 67
Mohawk, 80
Mont Blanc, 23–24
Morgan, Edward, 30, 31
Morgan, Linda, 30–32
Morning Dew (sailboat), 80
Moro, Hassan, 19
Morro Castle (cruise ship), 59
U.S. Congress acts after fire on, 80

National Geographic Society, 66
National Oceanic and Atmospheric Administration (NOAA), 39
National Transportation Safety Board (NTSB), 53, 61, 84
Go Team, 72–74
National Weather Service, 78
Neptune (ferry), 20
Normal Accidents: Living with High-Risk Technologies (Perrow), 11–12
S.S. *Noronic* (passenger cruiser), 81–82

Oceans Blue Foundation, 82
Oil Pollution Act (1990), 90
Oil Spill Intelligence Report, 90
oil spills, 88, 90–91, 91–92. *see also specific ships*
cleanup of, 92
oil tankers, 20–21, 26, 27, 34, 50
EU banning of single-hull, 92
phasing out older and substandard, 90, 95
rebuilding, 88, 90–91

The Perfect Storm (Junger), 58
Perrow, Charles, 11–12, 50
Phillips, Jack, 16–17
Prestige (oil tanker), 91–92
Preston, Diana, 65
Prince of Wales, 22
Princess May (passenger/cargo ship), 89
Princess Sophia, 34–35
Prinsendam (cruise ship), 85

Queen Mary (ocean liner), 14–15

radar, 29, 75, 76, 79, 95
The Raft of the Medusa (Gericault), 48
reefs, 14, 19, 39
Republic (ocean liner), 38, 86
rescue efforts, 28, 45
Andrea Doria, 33–34
Coast Guard search and, 42–43
early, 38–39
Eastland, 37–38
Rickover, Hyman G., 66
Robertson, Jim, 77–78
rogue waves, 14–15
roll-on/roll-off (ro-ro) ferries, 19, 56–57, 69–70, 72
improving, 86–88
issue of unsafe, 88
requirements for VDRs on, 75
Royal Caribbean Cruise Line, 83
Royal Majesty (cruise ship), 46

S-13 (submarine), 23
safety
in commercial fishing industry, 92–94
equipment, 40, 79
increased on cruise ships, 82–84
policies, and controlling ships' access to ports, 91
progress made in, 79
regulations and technological advances, 39
-related overhauls, 80
relation of flags of convenience to, 83
sinking of *Titanic*, as wake-up call for marine, 11
standards imposed on passenger ships, 80
Salem Express (ferry), 19

Saved! The Story of the Andrea Doria (Hoffer), 32
Scandinavian Star (cruise ship), 83
    difficulty of finding exits on, 84
Sea Empress (oil tanker), 27
Seafarer (tug/barge), 53–54
The Sea's Bitter Harvest (Campbell), 92–93
Shackleton, Ernest, 36
shipbuilding
    design flaws, 55–56
    evolution of, 13
    new technologies for, 58
    shoddy, 19, 55–56
ships
    danger associated with conversion of, 57–58
    early, 13
    evacuation of, 84–86, 89. *see also* lifeboats
    fires onboard, 40–41, 58, 59, 60, 61. *see also*
        cruise ships, fires onboard
    at mercy of weather, 13–15, 43, 45, 75–77
    operating under flags of convenience, 83
    phasing out older and substandard, 95
    refusal of docking privileges to, 91
shipwrecks
    causes of, 46–62
    contribution of nature to, 13–15, 43, 45
    human error and, 29–30, 45, 46, 48–50,
        53–54, 70, 77–78
    nonweather factors leading to, 15–17
    oil spills from, 26–27. *see also* oil spills
    reduction in common causes of, 79
    response to tragedies of, 79–80
    survival factors, 28, 38–40
Smith, Edward, 8, 15–16, 49
smoke detectors, 83–84
sonar, 75, 89
SOS (call for help), 16, 32–33, 34, 39, 52
Stockholm (ocean liner), 29–32, 34
Storstad (coal ship), 51–52, 71
Sultana (steamboat), 55–56, 58
    legislation instituted after boiler explosion
        on, 80

Taiho (aircraft carrier), 21
Talisman, 80
terrorist attacks (September 11, 2001), 25
Titanic (ocean liner), 8–10, 15–18, 28, 86
    accumulated errors involving, 48–50

issues addressed after sinking of, 80
    problems with construction of, 17–18
    shortage of lifeboats on, 9–10, 18
    sinking, as wake-up call for marine safety, 11
Torrey Canyon (oil tanker), 26, 88
Turner, William, 67, 68

U-20 (submarine), 65, 69
United Nations (UN), 70
Universe Explorer (cruise ship), 84
"Unsinkable": The Full Story of RMS Titanic
        (Butler), 49–50
U.S. Coast Guard, 11, 39, 45, 72, 78, 86
    investigations, 77–78
    recommendations for commercial fishing
        fleet, 94
    revamping of internal communication
        systems in, 80
    search-and-rescue facilities, 42–43
U.S. Congress, 80, 88, 90
U.S. Merchant Marine Act (1936), 80

Varghese, K.M., 61–62
Vestris (passenger steamer), 11
Victor (oil tanker), 20–21, 34
voyage data recorder (VDR), 75
Voyager of the Seas (cruise ship), 83

warships, 21–23
Western Electric Company, 35
White Star Line, 18
Wilhelm Gustloff (ocean liner), 23
wireless radio, 16–17
    importance of, 38
    necessity of continual coverage using, 80
    signals for help, 16
Womack, John, 57
World War I, 23, 64
    effect of *Lusitania* sinking on U.S. entry into,
        68
World War II, 21–23
*Wreck of the Medusa: The Tragic Story of the
        Death Raft* (McKee), 47

Yamato (battleship), 21
Yarmouth Castle (cruise ship), 82
    fire onboard, 40–41

Picture Credits

About the Author

Hillary Mayell writes science news stories for the *National Geographic* website on topics ranging from dinosaurs, the origins of humans, evolution, and ancient cultures, to the environment, conservation, and human rights issues. She and her family live in Sun Valley, Idaho.